Edition Angewandte
Buchreihe der Universität für angewandte Kunst Wien
Herausgegeben von Gerald Bast, Rektor

Universität für angewandte Kunst Wien
University of Applied Arts Vienna

Sonja Stummerer & Martin Hablesreiter

food design S_{mall}

Reflections on Food, Design and Language

Contributions by Susann Vihma and Fabio Parasecoli
Photos by Ulrike Köb and Daisuke Akita

DE GRUYTER

Editorial office and proofreading (German): Martin Hablesreiter
Translation: Alun Brown
Cover design and graphics: Martin Hablesreiter
Cover photography: honey & bunny, Ulrike Köb, www.koeb.at
Photographs: honey & bunny, Ulrike Köb, Daisuke Akita
Printing: gugler* print, A-Melk/Donau
Content and Production Editor on behalf of the Publisher:
Katharina Holas, A-Vienna
Project Management "Edition Angewandte" on behalf of the
University of Applied Arts Vienna: Roswitha Janowski-Fritsch, A-Vienna

Library of Congress Control Number: 2019955261

Bibliographic information published by the German National Library
The German National Library lists this publication in the Deutsche
Nationalbibliografie; detailed bibliographic data are available on the
Internet at http://dnb.dnb.de.

ISSN 1866-248X
978-3-11-067975-5

www.degruyter.com

Overall concept: Sonja Stummerer & Martin Hablesreiter
Research: Sonja Stummerer
Text: Sonja Stummerer
with contributions by Susann Vihma and Fabio Parasecoli

The book is based on ideas and hypotheses on "Food Design" that have been developed by Martin Hablesreiter and Sonja Stummerer (honey & bunny) over the past 15 years. Some of these ideas were published in the book "Food Design XL," Springer, 2010. The present book is a theoretical continuation of the topic, researched and written by Sonja Stummerer.

We would like to thank Gabriele Sorgo and Wilhelm Berger for their support.

We would like to thank Ulrike Köb and Daisuke Akita for kindly permitting the printing of the photographs.

www.koeb.at
www.daisukeakita.com

Kindly supported by MA 7; Stadt Wien

www.honeyandbunny.com

Contents

Some thoughts concerning food design and semiotics
Foreword by Susann Vihma

Food can be called a design object just like any other artifact. This conclusion is central to the book at hand. At first, the statement may seem a bit odd for the reader. However, the topic is elaborated and discussed in many ways. After reading the chapters it convinces of the necessity to talk about food design, especially if food is served as dishes or when food is presented as a product on a store shelf or conceived as recipes. Meat and vegetables consequently become designed. So, food can be approached in design research in order to better understand its specific and versatile meanings.

As an everyday necessity, food is undoubtedly highly placed as an object of interest for all of us. The book underlines that it is, nevertheless, not sufficient for us to consume food for nutrition, i.e., take in edible stuff for our biological needs. In addition, cultural aspects seem to be of utmost importance where eating is concerned, because food is served according to many traditions which people choose to follow all the time.

The book takes a closer look at the cultural meanings of food and design with the help of several approaches. Among these approaches are various semiotic theories which have already dealt with food earlier. And, even if food has not explicitly been the subject of most of these studies, semiotic concepts seem applicable to the analyses of food as well.

Interestingly, semiotic theories vary considerably according to their basic assumptions, particularly due to their conception of verbal language. In the book, the role of language with respect to ontology and epistemology is a crucial subject. The idea of analyzing verbal language by investigating its underlying structures goes back to the Saussurean semiotic tradition, which e.g., Roland Barthes follows in his systematic approach.[1] Barthes makes fascinating reading and offers many insights in his essays on the garment system and food system among many others. Max Bense, in his text, follows another tradition; i.e., the Peircean philosophy, which is founded on different assumptions.[2] Unfortunately, Charles Sanders Peirce (1839–1914) seems not to have been very well-known for various reasons. One of them is due to his written legacy, which was edited and published quite late. Some early applications of his philosophical ideas may have hampered their further use in design theory, because they were developed into formalized systems of interpretation. Schematic categories are created (Kawama Tetsuo[3]) and the taxonomy easily becomes a goal in itself. In Peirce s philosophy, the different modes (categories) of reference merge, however. In my view, the semiotic application worked out by Bense also tends towards a strict system of categories.[4] At the HfG Ulm, where he taught, semiotics was introduced among other new theoretical approaches considered useful for design purposes. The lectures by Tomás Maldonado at the Ulm school in the 1960s should also be mentioned here. He used semiotic concepts to enhance design methods and practice. He aimed at forming a universal visual language (visual symbols for technical products).

Semiotic approaches have been difficult to tackle in design discourses, in practice and in education. One promising approach is presented by Alvise Mattozzi, which he also implemented in his teaching in Italy.[5] Interestingly, this method applies yet another semiotic tradition, namely greimasian concepts.

But why are semiotic theories needed in design research in the first place? The answer depends on the research question at hand. What matters in research is to find the best ways to reach the goal, i.e., the ways that provide opportunities to proceed and arguments for worthy answers to the stated question. Klaus Krippendorff discards semiotics altogether without any interest in going into its potentials. He relies on other theoretical foundations in looking at design from a product semantic viewpoint.[6]

Various semiotic traditions, some of which have been mentioned above, have been popular and have offered ideas and concepts to discourses in other fields; for example in journalism and market-ing. Hence, we may bump into words like icon, metaphor, metonym, signal, sign, representation, and signification with different – often more or less vague – connotations as compared to elaborated semi-otic texts. These concepts are typical of semiotics, because its key focus lies in meaning formation processes and communication.

Some of the approaches concerning questions of design interpretation (semantics) stress the primary role of verbal language. Therefore, it is tempting to think of product language or design language, and even more broadly of visual language, i.e., conceive of design products as language-like objects, which form a kind of non-verbal language. Elements of verbal language are compared with and applied to visual matters and they are seen as communicating like verbal language does (form language tells the user, someone reads a picture). It follows that visual matters also need to be divided into units like words and letters in verbal language, and so on. However, as this book also points out, visual topics are not characterized by such a clear-cut and limited structure of units. On the contrary, visual units of objects cannot be divided universally according to an order (like grammatical rules), but must be discussed and defined according to the case at hand. Hence, it can be questioned whether there is a visual language (symbol system) in the first place. I have elsewhere discussed this dilemma and argued for the conception that it may be mislead-ing. It would be more helpful to accept the specific qualities of visual matters to begin with, and only then aim at finding idiosyncratic concepts and processes for visual analyses.[7] Interesting insights may come out looking closely at dining and dishes as visual metaphors, for example.

Food design is not only visual design, but incorporates other senses and it would be interesting to problematize the language aspects further. This book on food design asks why food is so varied and elaborated. It states that food is evaluated by means of its color, taste, smell, or texture, rather than through its shape. These characteristics belong to design. Naturally food is also evaluated through its biological factors, its effects on health. Food is design when feeding becomes a cultural act; e.g., dining and preparing dishes. Accordingly, food becomes an edible design object. In the specific case of a food object its materiality seems important to emphasize, also in semantic scrutiny. The Peircean approach observes this fact by introducing the indexical mode of the sign process, i.e. the causal relation to the reference (the object not only indicating its reference). In the book, materiality is dealt with in many significant ways.

The book brings forth the need to analyze food as a design object and interpret its symbolic qualities. People should be more aware of the various cultural meanings of food and how they are communicated, because food design influences our lives and can help solve environmental problems. It seems essential to promote the inclusion of the topic of food and design in design research.

Susann Vihma is professor emerita of Design History and Design Semiotics at the Department of Art at the Aalto University in Finland (in office between 2004 and 2013).

1   Barthes, Roland, Elements of Semiology, Hill and Wang, New York, 1968

2   Bense, Max, Zeichen und Design, Agis Verlag, Baden-Baden, 1971

3   https://researchmap.jp/read0030985/?lang=english (27.11.2019)

4   The book by Bense inspired me to begin with, because it offered an approach to design semantics, and at that time there were not many texts to study. However, it did not seem fruitful to apply the Bensean formalization, and I turned to the main primary sources, i.e., the writings of Charles S. Peirce.

5   Mattozzi, Alvise, Semiotic Analyses of Objects: a model, in: Vihma, Susann, Design Semiotics in Use, University of Art and Design, Helsinki, 2010, pp. 40–68

6   Krippendorff, Klaus, The Semantic Turn, Taylor & Francis, Boca Raton, 2006

7   https://www.researchgate.net/publication/284403746_Design_as_Language_a_Misconception (22.11.2019)

What is food design?
Foreword by Fabio Parasecoli

What is food design? This is the question that lies at the core of this book, in which Sonja Stummerer and Martin Hablesreiter (also known as the duo honey & bunny) share their considerations on how food is inevitably designed, and, as such, how it participates in dense networks of social communication.

Food design, as a burgeoning field of professional practice and academic research, is still relatively new. It now has its own scholarly publication, the International Journal of Food Design. A growing corpus of books, magazines, websites, and visual materials suggests that there is potential, both in terms of expert activities and public interest. I had the opportunity and the honor to be an external advisor for the Victoria and Albert Museum exhibition "Food: Bigger than the Plate," in which Sonja and Martin participated with their film "Food | RULES | tomorrow." Before the London show, the Triennale di Milano dedicated an exhibition to food during the 2015 Milan Expo, and so did MAXXI, the Museum of Contemporary Art in Rome. Various associations of different levels of activity have emerged, such as the Red LatinoAmericana de Food Design and Food Design North America, which provide a space to discuss, collaborate, and grow together.

I do not think there is a single answer to the question of what food design is. And maybe there should not be just one; at least not yet. Food design is growing, and growing fast, and it is not totally clear yet what it may actually be. Food Design North America, for instance, states that its goal is to "improve our relationship with food, individually or collectively, in the most diverse ways and instances. Its actions can relate to the design of food products, materials, practices, environments, systems, processes and experiences." Francesca Zampollo, founder of the International Food Design Society, has proposed a mapping of food design that identifies six subcategories: Design With

Food (focusing on "food as a raw material"), Design For Food ("design of all the products used to cut, chop, mix, contain, preserve, store, cook and present food"), Food Space Design or Interior Design For Food, Food Product Design ("design of food to be mass produced"), Design About Food ("design of objects inspired by food," which highlights symbolic meanings of products"), and Eating Design ("design process for any eating situation where there are people interacting with food"). Of course, there are practitioners and researchers who would not fit in this taxonomy, which some may find too restrictive and limiting. This variety of theoretical approaches and practical attitudes is also reflected in how food design gets linked to cultural and social issues, production and consumption modalities, use of objects and space, communal well-being, and musings about the future and the impact of technology.

Those who claim food design as their professional world probably feel a greater need to define it. As a non-designer and a food studies researcher who collaborates with designers both in reflecting about theories and methodologies and in participating in applied projects, what is important to me is not so much elaborating a univocal and final definition of food design, but rather understanding why we are even talking about food design, how and why it emerged, how it connects to the developments within design at large, and why it is emerging at this specific historical point in time. There may not be any firm answers yet, but it is quite likely that food design is a manifestation of the overall growing interest in food and the acknowledgment of its centrality in human life. Improving the global food system in terms of sustainability, justice, and attention to human needs rather than prioritizing business and profit, is now identified as one of the great challenges that humankind is facing and on which it is staking its survival.

Against this background, Sonja Stummerer and Martin Hablesreiter propose a reflection that, as often happens with good and stimulating thoughts, poses questions instead of providing answers.

At the beginning, they wonder whether "food can be considered a design object in the same way as electrical appliances, cars, or furniture." This is a central issue because food, unlike other objects of design, is incorporated into us through the act of ingestion, and it is entangled since infancy in the emotional and psychological dynamics that contribute to the construction of individual and social identities. Furthermore, Stummerer and Hablesreiter point out that food can be considered as a form of non-verbal language which carries layers of meaning. If this is the case, what is the role of design in shaping those meanings through interventions on forms and function, on aesthetic elements like texture and visual aspect, as well as on how dishes and products are produced, distributed, and consumed? And if design is about change and innovation, especially as part of contemporary consumer culture which puts a premium on novelty, how does it relate to tradition and history?

Having known Stummerer and Hablesreiter for several years now, I know their book has taken shape within a professional activity expressing itself through performances, exhibitions, and museum pieces that address urgent questions: How can food designers present new behaviors to consumers? How can they move from ideas and projects to actual production? What is the best way of introducing daring, paradigm-shifting innovation into the food industry, which is often hesitant to take risks and ends up proposing more of the same, often just in larger quantities? And how can these innovations become part of larger cultural and social visions? As I said at the beginning, so many questions – all valid and important – emerge from Stummerer's and Hablesreiter's discussion of food design and its ethical aspects.

Stummerer's and Hablesreiter's interest in food started during their studies of architecture at the Universität für angewandte Kunst (University of Applied Arts) in Vienna, under the mentorship of Hans Hollein. In the 1976 exhibition "Man Transforms" at the Cooper Hewitt National Design Museum in New York City, Hollein placed the human body at the center of a far-reaching reflection on space, tools, and behaviors, which inevitably led him to food. On that occasion, Hollein focused on bread from all over the world to reflect on how something so basic also has so much design applied to it. Many years later, inspired by their mentor's inquiries, Stummerer and Hablesreiter started exploring the forms and functions of common foods and eating implements, as well as their origins and development over time. Fish sticks were as intriguing to them as the traditional breads or Japanese tea sweets with which they familiarized themselves during a year-long stint in Japan working as architects.

In this book, Stummerer and Hablesreiter fall back on design practice and theory, philosophy, and semiotics in trying to make sense of food design in general but also their own professional path. In developing their arguments, they refer to several authors that are not necessarily well known in the English-speaking world, thus providing fresh material for reflection. This volume constitutes a thoughtful contribution to a new field that at times, due to enthusiasm and the urgency of the issues it deals with, lacks in reflexivity. One can only hope that others will follow Stummerer's and Hablesreiter's example in assessing and evaluating what they do through attentive and critical eyes.

Fabio Parasecoli is Professor of Food Studies in the Nutrition and Food Studies Department at New York University. His scholarly work explores food, popular culture, and politics, particularly in food design and food heritage. His last book "Food" (2019) was published by MIT Press as part of the Essential Knowledge series.

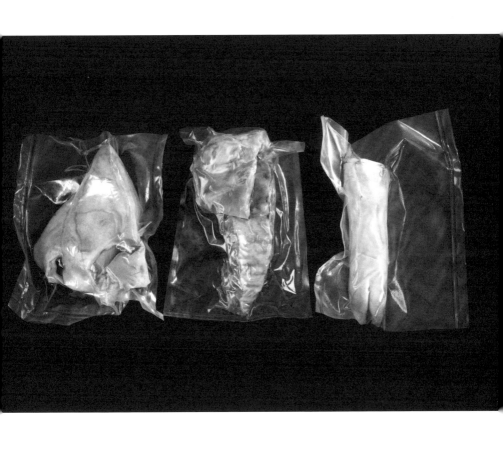

Introduction

More than a thousand times per year, before each meal, we select, slice, heat up, stir and mix in other words design raw commodities and basic produce into dishes and foods. Whether pastry or pasta, frozen vegetables or confectionery: everything has to be prepared and designed in the "right" way before being fit for consumption. But can food be considered a design object in the same way as electrical appliances, cars or furniture?

The need to process and shape food is as old as civilization.[1] "In terms of cultural history, preparing dishes the provision of food to people is even older than architecture, the very provider of shelter from the cold and rain. In other words, it is mankind's oldest form of artistic expression. Cooking, like all other forms of art, expresses the worldview of a civilization."[2]

The idea of getting to grips with the design of food came to us as we were doing a year of work experience as architects in Tokyo. The elaborate and detailed presentation of Japanese food fascinated us. On the other hand, however, we came to the understanding that it was impossible for a cultural stranger to decode, let alone understand, the meanings and messages that lay behind these designs. This experience inspired us to question our own culture's food, with which we had been so familiar since childhood and which we thought we knew intimately. Why are dishes and drinks served at the table in THIS form and not in another? And what are the reasons behind these particular design processes?

Every year, roughly 50,000 new food products are released worldwide on the market, of which only a little more than half are still available more than a year later.[3] What motivates people to prepare, shape and present food in a certain way? Why are some styles still around after 2000 years, while others only last 2 months? How does food have to be designed so that it is successful in a cultural rather than an economical sense?

Food products as a blind spot in design research

"Why does food have to be designed? For the same reason that furniture, clothing or surgical instruments are designed."[4]

Food Design is one of the more neglected areas within design research. While collaboration with designers is commonplace in order to develop radios, bicycles or mobile phones, this process of professionalization in food design has not yet happened. Comestibles with a few exceptions tend to be served without the involvement of any designers. This being the case, can food products be considered design objects at all, and to what extent can design theory be applied to the subject of food?

Food and dishes are indeed not merely physical material objects; they are also – if produced or prepared by humans – design objects whose attributes, whether taste, smell, texture or other object properties, are determined during the design process. This presents us with some room to maneuver. If food even seemingly "natural" food is thought of as being formed by humans, the manner of its design can likewise be tampered with. The what and the how, as well as the intended principles and goals, can be reflected on and (consciously) changed. From an economic point of view, this type of thinking and research already takes place in the field of marketing; though rarely in terms of cultural, socio-political or social goals.

This book addresses a hitherto little-discussed aspect of food; namely that of design. It examines where the forms (styles) of our food come from and which factors play a role in the process of its design, from the selection of the ingredients through processing up to consumption. The second part of the book, based on the theories of the American philosopher Susanne Langer, deals with theoretical considerations of how objects function as elements of a non-verbal language and uses edible examples to show how certain aesthetic characteristics can be linked with meanings, abstract contents and symbolic universes.

The book attempts at a further understanding of the origins and significance of food and dishes, and to answer the question of how the shape or appearance of food is used as a form of expression to convey content and store knowledge. The theme is presented as a work of literature which uses hermeneutic and phenomenological means to answer the questions posed, and is aimed at designers. The focus here is neither on the empirical nor on the historical, but on the inclusion of comestibles as design objects in the context of design sciences.

We hope that exploring food as an object of design contributes to examining the very qualities of food. In the vast majority of cases, people choose whether or not to eat a specific something for emotional rather than rational reasons. They respond to the symbolism of food and the ideas it evokes in them. Awareness about the meanings that food conveys helps to understand and reflect the traditions and predefined values which have an important role in eating; not merely to follow them blindly, but to question, adapt and, if necessary, discard them. Shapes can be used for manipulative purposes, and meals and dishes can be misused as ideological tools. On the other hand, knowing about objects and their cultural meanings enables the continuous examination and evolution of the culture (of food). It furthermore empowers consumers – in this case the people eating – in a very political sense toward self-determination or co-determination.

We have published three books on the subject of food and design: "Food Design, von der Funktion zum Genuss," Springer, 2005, "Food Design XL," Springer, 2010 and "Eat Design," Metro Verlag, 2013. "Food Design Small" is now an attempt to piece together and expand upon theoretical foundations for the theses developed therein.

1   See Barlösius, 1999, p. 14
2   Kubelka, 2004, p. 15
3   See Prahl, Setzwein, 1999, p. 227
4   Guixé, 2010, p. 113

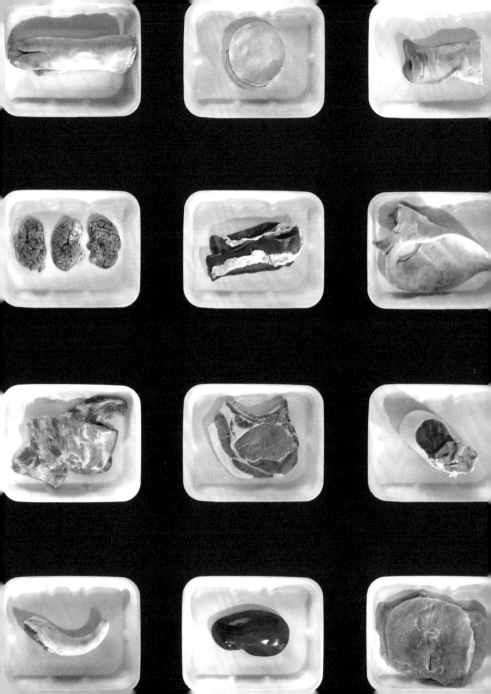

Food and Design

Of all the abundance of food that is naturally grown, only the tiniest percentage reaches the plate raw and whole. Most of it is processed in one way or another before we put it in our mouths. Food is peeled, cut, split, blended, boiled, fried, whipped and frozen: Food is designed. "Food makes its transformation from mere fuel to something meaningful through the careful combination of tastes, textures, odors, colors and shapes. There are distinct parallels between cooking and design."[1] It doesn't matter if it is fruit, grain or meat: Raw produce is processed in order to make it enjoyable and tasty, to preserve it or to transport it.[2]

Design?

There has been a great deal of debate and work written about what "design" is and what it isn't. It nonetheless first seems necessary to briefly address the terms "design" and "form" in order to clarify what they mean or can mean with regard to food and food design. Can the term "design," in the usual sense of the word, even be applied to food?

The question of what design is and what it isn't is not an easy one to answer, because "design" is an everyday term rather than a scientific one. Etymologically, it is derived from the Latin "designare" which means "designate," "indicate," "determine" or even "define," "describe," or "mark out."[3] "The etymology of design goes back to the Latin de + signare, marking out, setting apart, giving significance by assigning it to a use, user, maker or owner."[4] In the Italian Renaissance, the initial concept of a work of art, i.e., the plan, the sketch or the fundamental idea, was called "disegno interno." In contrast, "disegno esterno" stood for the finished work. In 1588, the Oxford English Dictionary included the term "design" and described it as a man-made plan, schema, or the design sketch of a work of art, but also as an object of applied art.[5]

Food and Design

The "Design Dictionary" by Erlhoff and Marshall (2008) describes "design" as a goal-oriented transformation process that intervenes in the environment, leading to its deliberate alteration.[6] Both of these are also applicable to the production and preparation of food, because when people eat they don't just directly eat raw materials; they also process them into products and dishes that are prepared and designed in a specific style and manner. Ingredients are kneaded into doughs, which are in turn formed not only into simple flat-breads, but are also folded into pretzels, braids or bagels and bent into crescent-shaped croissants. If cheese is poured into cylindrical loaves and chocolate into square slabs, fish cut into geometric blocks, and cornmeal porridge is shaped into peanut curls, then food is designed – quite deliberately and according to specific criteria.[7]

Food can be thought of as "designed" in the true sense of the word because both the cooking and the industrial processing of food are concerned with deliberate, goal-oriented processes that have the clear intention of bringing about a specific change in the environment (i.e., its ingredients). As a three-dimensional, physical-material object, food that has been processed by human beings comes under the subject of   product design. Food that is designed by people can there-fore be analyzed as an object of design research. As design and design research are intrinsically interdisciplinary in nature, design research would even seem to be a promising and appropriate way of research-ing food that is being taken on as a research topic in both the natural sciences as well as in various humanities.

When we talk about food design, we mean all deliberate (i.e., brought about with a specific aim in mind) altering of objects in the surrounding environment (nature). This kind of purpose-orientated design actually begins with the breeding of more productive or more resilient varieties and breeds.

However, food differs in some ways from "classic" design objects such as furniture, electrical appliances or vehicles. Contrary to many other items, food (even on a conscious level) is largely evaluated not through its shape but through other characteristics such as color, taste, smell, or texture. Hence, the difference in the way the word "design" is used in daily language on the one hand and in a professional sense on the other is particularly clear as regards food. Whereas in daily language design is often associated with decoration, style or visual appearance, the professional use of the word design not only means giving an object an appearance or shape, but also a materiality, a function, a meaning and so on. Not only does design determine the external appearance of the object in question, but also all its attributes, e.g., how it works, how it sounds, how it smells or how it tastes. Design determines the quality of an object or thing.

The view of design as the conscious modification of the aesthetic appearance of things, information, etc.,[8] is misleading because physical objects have no appearance besides the aesthetic. Were this the case, they would be shapeless (without form) and could be neither communicated nor perceived. Because we are only able to perceive through the senses, the perception and determination of aesthetic attributes is the only way of perceiving our surroundings or even interacting with the outside world. The aesthetic appearance of an object is therefore not just something that is added to it, but is an inherent part of the object itself that cannot be altered independently of it. In other words: If you change the aesthetic appearance of an object, you change the object itself.

Food and its "form"

The "form" in which food comes to the table is a question of design – in both senses of the word. In artistic terms, "form" is understood in the direct, material sense to be an outline, or a material boundary – without taking into account the meaning of the content in question. The "form" of a thing thus means the true physical shape in which something appears. In the context of product design for example, "form" is understood to be the material, malleable shape of an object that is physically manifest; i.e., the specific geometry of a real object in space. On the other hand, figuratively speaking – which is also relevant in design – "form" describes the mode of representation (for example the form a text or piece of music takes) or the (abstract) structuring of ideas and meanings. Basically, both interpretations always apply to an object: A dish or meal "has" a form and it "is" a form. A donut or muffin has a particular (physical) form, but at the same time they are also a form in which a sweet is prepared. The Finnish design theorist Susann Vihma describes "form" as the association between a material object and the representations (ideas and symbols, for example) generated by its perception and interpretation. She argues that the relation between material structure and these representations can be called "form". Form therefore has a double meaning.[9]

The double meaning of "form" often leads to misunderstandings in the field of design. This is because the design of an object not only determines its physical form, but also its overall quality and thereby all the other attributes of the object in question as well, such as its materiality, the quality of how it feels, its sound, its smell or its outward appearance (e.g., if it is dull, shiny, reflective, porous, soft, etc.). Since three-dimensional objects are experienced with all five senses, the perceptions of all senses contribute to their appearance. Conversely, physical-material form is directly perceived by the senses of sight and touch and only indirectly by hearing. The smell and taste of an object either barely contributes to its material form or not at all. Especially in the case of food, which is primarily experienced from within the body, the overall impression given by its physical form tends to take a back seat compared to other properties, because we can only feel, but not see, inside the body. Food products are experienced among other things as being about the flavor, the aroma, the chewing sounds, the texture, its relative toughness or tenderness, and what it feels like in the mouth; its physical form plays a rather subordinate role in comparison to these abovementioned perceptions. Even though the visual impression given by a type of food does contribute to its taste, it is – depending on the nature of the food – really more influenced by its color than by its shape. The impression given by colour stimulates certain (learned) anticipated tastes in the brain, which can be so strong that it can influence the actual perceived taste and even override it.

The "right form" for vegetables?

Apart from these two meanings, one direct and one figurative in nature, the word "form" also contains a moral component: the question of the "right" form. In design, the word is also associated with the historical and ideologically influenced concept of "good form", which is related to functionalism. Certainly, the early Werkbund objects that were aesthetically simple – i.e., designed to be functionally and socially useful, without decoration – were considered to be "good."[10] This definition demonstrates the ideological imprint and the (intentional) moral dimension of the "good form": because what passes as socially meaningful or functional can naturally only be determined in the context of a certain worldview.

"Good form" was intended to be a guiding principle for the design of all kinds of everyday objects, which did not at that time include food products. The design of certain foods, e.g., frozen vegetables, was nonetheless also influenced. The rejection of any form of decoration led among other things to somewhat more unnatural designs in the world of food products: because natural (e.g., floral) shapes – which were also in contrast to the angularity in fashion at that time – could be thought of as decoration, vegetables for example were chopped up into abstract cubes as part of the deep-freezing process. The design of carrots and turnips as frozen vegetables diced into small cubes, however, makes little sense with its abstract geometry (another ideal of "good form"). The ergonomic quality of such a product cuts both ways, however: although being eaten in small pieces is an advantage when using cutlery, e.g., spoons, the chopped vegetable pieces can't be held so easily – like for example a whole carrot can – and eaten by hand. Whether the design of frozen vegetables into small cubes is simple, functional, appropriate for the product and timeless, and of greater or lesser practical use, cannot be answered without an adequate reference system (value system, ideology). From today's perspective, the answer would probably be negative even though there is undeniably a certain timelessness about the product.

Food as product or industrial design

Western industrialized countries mass-produce a varying amount of food today, depending on the region. "Today, food is a mass-produced consumer commodity, and as such has as much claim to be a designed object as the Ford motor car. Ready meals, for example, go through much the same process of development as new industrial products."[11] Food is an exception, however, with regard to the professionalization of its design. Although all kinds of dishes and drinks are now being mass-produced on an industrial scale, from baked goods to ready meals to ice cream, confectionery and beverages, their design has not yet been professionalized. The temporal and personal disconnection from design and production accordingly took place as the production of food transitioned from artisanal to industrial. Design is not undertaken by designers, however, but by other professionals; e.g., by food technicians, chefs, chemists, entrepreneurs, or people in marketing. This situation is also astonishing because the industrial production of food started right at the beginning of the Industrial Revolution and there is even a causal connection between them, industrialization having led to a sudden increase in the urban population, which was of course cut off from the traditional way of producing food; namely agriculture. As a result, the demand for nutritious, cheap and easy-to-consume food for the growing urban population and the working class necessitated the industrial production of food as early as the mid-nineteenth century. The first production line in history was not found as is often told in the factories of Henry Ford, but in Chicago's slaughterhouses. There are numerous examples of early industrially manufactured food products, including among others: soluble, roller-dried milk powder (invented in 1855 by John A. Just), condensed milk (invented in 1856 by Gail Borden), Liebig's meat extract, the precursor of today's stock cube or bouillon cube (invented in 1862 by Justus von Liebig), margarine (invented in 1869 by Hippolyte Mège-Mouriès), vanillin (invented in 1874 by Wilhelm Haarmann), Cornflakes (invented in 1876 by John Harvey Kellogg or in 1906 by Will Keith Kellogg) or instant soup (invented in 1886 by Julius Maggi and Carl Knorr).[12]

1   Catterall, 1999, p. 23

2   See Stummerer, Hablesreiter, 2010, p. 8

3   See Erlhoff, Marshall , 2008, keyword design

4   Krippendorf, 2007, p. 69

5   See Bürdek, 1991, p. 13

6   See Erlhoff, Marshall, 2008, keyword design

7   See Stummerer, Hablesreiter, 2010, p. 8

8   See Erlhoff, Marshall, 2008, keyword design

9   See Vihma, 1997, p. 35

10   See Schneider, 2009, pp. 112–113

11   Catterall, 1999, p. 23

12   See Birus, 2000, p. 98

Food as a design object

Food is a basic physical need, a prerequisite of survival. In addition to its biological function, food is also a cultural, social and ritual staple of human existence. In the context of food design, however, another, new way of looking at food emerges: As an object. This perspective may seem strange – perhaps even challenging – at first, as it places the object as the center of attention rather than the eater. However, this by no means disparages food, but quite to the contrary is an opportunity to gain new insights into the ancient phenomenon – and most essential object in our environment – food.

What is food (substance)?

Along with breathing, the most intimate and direct contact we all experience with the external world is through eating. Each of us consumes around 75 tons of fluid and solid substances over the course of our lives.[1] This is partly digested – i.e., converted into the body's own substance – and partly excreted. With eating this assimilation happens by synthesizing bodily substances from nutrients. This is how the object – the food – relates to the subject – the eater. Viewed purely physically, the process of eating is a merging with the object;[2] that is, with the food you consume. From its first brush with the lips to its digestion by stomach acids, contact with food is therefore not only sensory, but also a profoundly personal, spiritual bodily experience: we become what we eat (and drink).[3] Our bodies are made up of what they have incorporated over the past few years; that is, in the period in which practically all the cells of the body have been renewed at least once. In material terms, people are the products of food.

Comestibles are therefore not just food objects, but foreign bodies that are assimilated into your own body. "Assimilation means the association of the eater with the eaten. One is constantly confronted with the danger of being transformed into what one acquires through eating. This makes eating a 'type of acquisition' in which what is acquired [the food] is transformed in the metabolic process."[4]

The contradiction inherent in food being a foreign invader from the external world on the one hand and being integrated into the individual body's interior life on the other strikes people everyday mostly as a result that they view their food as a mere carrier of nutrients and calories. Like a kind of fuel, it provides the energy needed to maintain vital functions; but rather than being integrated into the body, it "flows" through it instead. If one only regards food as a provider but not as a building block of the body, then there is no danger of being transformed by what one has consumed.[5]

People like to delude themselves that there is a blurring of the individual, of the independent self in the process of eating and digesting: "the relationship between the nourishing, eating Self and the eaten, incorporated Other."[6] Food is not merely a source of energy, but is also the "other" Self, that part of the outside world that is integrated into the Self through the process of eating. Hence, food occupies a special position within the world of objects, as it is more than just groceries or delicatessens, but is instead a fundamental part of the process of self-manifestation; this is what makes food and drink fundamentally different from other non-edible objects. The selection, preparation and releasing of food into the body not only means appropriating and incorporating a part of the world,[7] but also distinguishing oneself from the environment. The eater "takes possession of" the eaten objects; if they lose power over what they have ingested, they are threatened with the loss of their own identity.[8]

This way of looking at things places enormous value on food as an object. Within the elaborate selection, preparation and design of food, another level of understanding can be found: one which is not only socio-cultural, but also self-actualizing or self-designing in which the designed food items are the building blocks of one's own ego – not only in the transmitted, but also in the physical-material sense. The effort, attention, aims, actions and objectives that are directed towards the food during its processing and design are also a process of designing oneself: "The wielding of things is also a form of self-creation."[9] – In a sense that is as real as it is figurative. The things we surround ourselves with, as well as the style and manner in which we design, use, treat, or interact with these things, express our personality, lifestyle, and culture, and contribute to how we design ourselves and our lives. With food, and in contrast to other everyday objects, this self-actualization takes place not only symbolically, but also in a real, physical sense.

Eating can therefore be regarded as the formation of one's Self in a very concrete sense. The German pedagogue Werner Wiater even describes a possible connection between the Latin word "educare" (extract, raise, discipline) with "edere" (eat, rear). Originally, the word "education" may have referred to the raising of plants, animals and humans, and thus may have generally meant the cultivation of living beings through eating.[10]

With dietary supplements, medical or functional food, a physical self-actualization process takes place through eating, for instance. Functional food is synthetically enhanced with additional properties, e.g., so that it has a health-promoting, cholesterol-lowering, immune-boosting or digestion-promoting effect.[11] Functional foods are especially designed to have specific (desired) effects beyond those offered by the traditional purpose of eating, namely for bodily nourishment. They are ingested with the purpose of altering the state of the body. Examples of functional foods are vitamin-enriched, micro-nutrient or high-fiber beverages, snack bars or breakfast cereals, products with protein or amino acid additives, probiotic yoghurt, isotonic sports drinks, iodized table salt,[12] chewing gum with soy protein (to combat high cholesterol levels) and confectionery fortified with iron.[13] Even more apparent is how bodybuilders, who follow an extremely protein-rich diet with the express goal of sculpting the body in a very specific way, consciously design their bodies with the aid of nutrition.

Viewed from such a self-design perspective, the notion of food design opens up an enormous scope for creative freedom in everyone, because designing one's own food means having the power to design oneself. In reality, however, this individual freedom is conflicted by cultural conventions and is severely limited by social power and hier-archical structures.

What is food: culturally?

The question "What is food?" has of course a cultural dimension alongside the linguistic and the psychological. What is and is not "food" is defined differently in different cultures. Not all naturally edible things are eaten in every culture. On the contrary, each culture devises its own food menu or dietary plan, and labels anything edible that lies outside this set of rules as a food taboo or considers it disgusting.

Classifying the environment into "edible" and "inedible"

When infants, at around the age of one, indiscriminately put anything that crosses their paths into their mouths in order to feel and inspect it – literally to "grasp" it, they still don't know how to classify the objects of their surroundings into "edible" and "inedible." At this stage, they eat stones, sand or grass, and would without hesitation also put fecal matter into their mouths and swallow, were they not prevented from doing so. In the ensuing months and years, children then go through an enormous learning process: they learn that Lego bricks, teddy bears and chair legs fundamentally differ in one respect from cookies, bread crusts and banana mush: The latter can and should be put in the mouth and swallowed. At first, children examine the more appropriate eating objects in the same way as they do with a building block or a toy duck, with an unbiased and equally playful curiosity, by placing the object in the mouth and then gagging it out again. In time, they adopt the externally observed and sanctioned classification of the environment into "edible" and "inedible." They learn to distinguish food from other objects – thereby going through one of the first and most fundamental socialization processes.

This process, in which a culture-specific approach towards objects is learned, first takes place via parental sanctioning, then through the recognition of parental guidelines as part of an overarching system of social rules, and leads to a contemplation of and response to these obligations.[14] Looked at in this way, objects and the attitude towards them form an important building block in the development (formation) of the personality, contributing to collective-immediate socialization or to the adoption (or rejection) of the selfsame symbolic fabric of meaning (which is conveyed through the objects)[15] Food plays a particularly central role in socialization, because it serves as a projection screen of collective data and meaning and thus contributes towards integration into a group. This is because what is and what is not food is not biologically fixed but is a question of definition, which is made by social groups and then subsequently reviewed and adapted over and over again. There is no freedom from food, but there is certainly freedom in food,[16] as man's biological constitution does not tell him where to sexually relax and what he should eat.[17] Although biology dictates that we eat, it provides no indication – with few exceptions such as toxic substances - as to how we satisfy this need.[18] "What counts as food and what doesn't, is culturally determined by man."[19]

The relative reality of what is edible

In their book "The Social Construction of Reality,"[20] the Austrian-American sociologists Thomas Luckmann (b. 1927 in Aßling, today

Slovenia) and Peter L. Berger (b. 1929 in Vienna) developed a complex theory based on the notion of reality being socially constructed. "Reality" is defined as the quality of phenomena that exist irrespective of our will, and which cannot be wished away.[21] This theory is thus relevant to design because it conceives the world or reality as being designed, and hence designable, by man.

As a consequence, this socially "prescribed" living environment not only encompasses thinking and acting, but also very basic needs, particularly nutrition and sexuality: "social reality determines not only activity and consciousness but, to a considerable degree, organismic functioning."[22] The reality of food is also socially determined, because food does not exist as an absolute reality independent of man, but must always be defined in terms of such. Plants and animals themselves are not yet "food," only man makes them such. Among other things, this process is characterized by ritual, religious, social, hygienic, legal, etc. codes and values and is only minimally concerned with physical needs.[23] This practice of selecting food can also be regarded as part of "Food Design," because it "designs" the reality of food and forms an integral part of eating culture.

The range of animals and plants accepted as food varies greatly depending on region, social status, ethnicity, etc. and is subject to constant changes and adjustments. What we eat – and what we don't – is an expression of our socialization and social allegiance. Nutritional choices, as well as certain forms of preparation, form part of a collective consciousness, providing peoples and social and religious groups with a sense of identity.[24] For example, there is no biological reason for eating shrimp in Central Europe, but locust is generally shunned; fried rabbit is fine but the same treatment of cat or guinea pig is considered disgusting. "While both sexuality and nutrition are grounded in biological drives, these drives are extremely plastic in the human animal."[25] Humans are physically capable of eating what kills them. This occurs unconsciously when food is consumed that is poisoned, polluted, contaminated or rotten. But we also consciously eat food that is toxic: In Japan, for instance, the partially poisonous Fugu (Puffer Fish) is a particular specialty. Preparing it takes special skills, as the intestines, liver, ovaries and skin contain the deadly poison tetrodotoxin and so must not be damaged during cooking. The poison induces a state of intoxication, but a higher concentration can lead to paralysis and even death. The preparation of Fugu is therefore only permitted by appropriately trained and licensed chefs, nevertheless fatal incidents keep occurring – especially in private homes.[26] Another example of the voluntary consumption of toxic substances – to the point of death, in extreme cases – is alcohol poisoning. A properly socialized person, however, will feel disgusted at the sight of the "wrong" food,[27] such as a dog in a cooking pot.

The reality of food is therefore man-made and not a natural reality. The subdivision of the environment into "edible" and "non-edible" is not a biological imperative in the vast majority of cases, but a cultural construct, since the selection of food – with a few exceptions such as poisonous plants – is always relative (constructed) and not absolute (biologically predetermined). From the range of natural substances that are edible, some food types are chosen according to self-made criteria in keeping with one's respective worldview. These choices have developed through history, characterized by habits, traditions and external circumstances and ultimately reflect structures of power and belief; that is, each group's own constructions of meaning. Members of these groups subsequently see the choices they make – that is, the variety of foodstuffs deemed edible by a particular group – as the only valid and universal types of food there are, as if its existence was independent in spite of having been singled out beforehand. "But we remain unconscious of this construct and naively believe that it exists independently of us."[28] These observations are encountered not only with the choice of food but also its design, i.e., food design as a whole.

Ingesting and eating something is a psychological as well as a bodily process. Both the eye and the brain are with us as we eat.

Consciously or unconsciously, when it comes to food people abide by traditions, customs and rituals in order to – as civilized beings – set themselves apart from how animals eat. By adhering to them, ingesting food becomes a cultural act: Feeding becomes dining. These unwritten laws of eating also determine what we put in our mouths – and what we don't. Hardly any other aspect of life is as determined by ideals, rules and conventions as food. Lemke states "that food is, as it were, a normatively mined area and its [note: the methodology of Gastrosophy] ultimately unjustifiable truth is socially hotly contested."[29] That some people rigorously adhere to a cultural definition of what "food" is derives among other things from a certain deep-seated need to belong to a group, because not conforming to the general rules of eating behavior means disrespecting the values upon which they are based, and even the religious milieus with which they are associated.[30] Some examples of such violations are, e.g., art projects in which the artists make blood sausage out of their own blood (among others the Viennese artists' group Monochrome in 2003 or the British artist Marc Quinn in 1994[31]), or produce cheese from breast milk. These foods are a clear taboo within current Anglo-American-European food culture.

Who declares objects to be food?

The process that makes some parts of our surroundings (nature) "food" is mostly conventionally driven and is only to a small extent individual. How do these traditions emerge, i.e. who or what determines what food is and what it is not? "Reality is socially defined. But the definitions are always embodied, that is, concrete individuals and groups of individuals serve as definers of reality. To understand the state of the socially constructed universe at any given time, or its change over time, one must understand the social organization that permits the definers to do their defining."[32]

One such social institution which determines our nutritional reality and legitimizes it as appropriate are food codes in modern constitutional states, which specifically define what may and may not be marketed as food and also how these food items have to be produced – or designed. So for example the Austrian Food Code in the chapter on meat and meat-based products clearly identifies which parts of a slaughtered animal are "meat" (and which are not) and provides detailed instructions, sometimes even diagrams, of how to section the carcasses and cut them into standard marketable cuts of meat.[33]

Another example is the European Union's Novel Food Regulations. These regulate the growing list of what is officially accepted as food within the EU by determining which food products by their nature are "new" or culturally alien (i.e., "Novel Food"), and under what conditions they may be marketed. According to them, for example, "new food" would include high-pressure pasteurized tomato puree, certain meat substitutes and products produced by means of high-pressure sterilization, high-voltage preservation or genetic engineering. The calorie-free fat substitute Olestra R, a sucrose polyester with fatty acids made of soybean, corn and cottonseed oil, is also labeled a Novel Food.[34] Exotic fruits or meats that are not common in Europe can also be included, however.[35] These "new" foods have to undergo an approval procedure before they can be placed on the market and are subject to special labeling requirements.[36]

It is interesting to note how the regulations define "new" food. In order to create a distinction between "conventional" and "novel" food, a specific point in time was established to help differentiate between them. Thus, everything that was not "used for human consumption to any significant extent" before 1997 is "new." This distinction makes little sense in terms of content, because whatever was produced before 1997 – regardless of how it was produced – is seen as a "traditional product"; and whatever was not consumed to any significant extent (in the EU) is conversely seen as "new" or at least "exotic." The regulation has thus indirectly given itself the task of being the determinant of European food culture. That this distinction between "conventional" and "new" food products is entirely fabricated, the vague definition of which ("significant extent") allowing plenty of room for interpretation, is also reflected in the existence of the so-called Novel Food catalog. When in doubt, the European Commission has to decide on a case-by-case basis whether a foodstuff or an ingredient has been "consumed to any significant extent" and whether it falls under the Novel Food Regulation or not. This catalog contains a list of all decisions concerning this matter on the Commission's website. The catalog is one of the institutions that determines the world of food for EU citizens.

How the food of a given group is chosen is – as has already been mentioned – not a natural process for the most part, but is socially constructed and represents at the same time a group-specific, symbolic universe. Laws represent one possible way of legitimizing this choice, in that they sanction violations and only allow limited changes to the system. The European Union's Novel Food Regulations impede or limit the increase in available food types. From an economic perspective, the regulations primarily show a preference for large companies, since the approval procedures are elaborate and therefore very expensive. Small and medium-sized businesses are thus limited in their opportunities for innovation.

Food as an object

When one considers food in terms of design, it is not in the foreground either as a biological, psychological or social phenomenon, but in its characteristic as a material object. In a literal sense, the term "object" refers to something contradictory. In everyday life, an object is a (smaller, harder) kind of item, a thing not described in detail. Essentially, an object can denote anything that has a fixed shape and is not a living being; that is, offers (at least some) resistance when touched.

A material object offers resistance to the body or part of the body and opposes one's own freedom of movement. It can be experienced with the senses and is typically not alive. The German youth educator Donata Elschenbroich mentions the unwieldy "alternative universe of objects – a daily obstacle course."[37] When a blind man walks through a forest and bumps into the trees, he experiences it as as physical resistance, a negative place with regard to his own freedom of movement. He experiences the object "tree" in the original sense of the term object: as an obstacle that opposes his movement and what he is trying to do; namely walk through the forest.[38]

In a broader sense, an object is anything that can be distinctively referred to using words. The term is not limited to external, material objects, but includes everything that can be named or bestowed with properties.[39]

Strictly speaking, the term material object can be used to describe basically everything that can be detected by touch and is not a living being. In daily speech, an object usually does not exceed a certain size (it is usually smaller than the toucher) and is in a solid state or phase. An ice cube is an object in everyday language, but a drop of water is not, even though it is physically the same substance. Since this common distinction over the physical state doesn't hold under greater scrutiny, among other things because there is no clear dividing line between liquid and solid foods such as mashed potatoes or goulash, when we speak of edible objects, we also include liquid and viscous foods such as soups, creams or mousses and likewise gaseous dishes as long as they are perceived as standalone dishes or foods.

Examples of gaseous foods can be found in e.g., molecular cuisine. Here, "air" refers to a separate category of gaseous foods that are served in special vessels, by means of bellows or a spray bottle, or as incense sticks. Another example of gaseous food is Catalan designer Martí Guixé's "Pharma-food" project of 1999, which allows food to be inhaled. In Pharma-bars or from bottles, differently flavored or composed (e.g., boiled beef formula P1) mixtures of microparticles containing nutrients and calories are inhaled. A special substance, the "saliva activator," ensures that these particles stick to the moisture within the throat and thus land in the digestive tract rather than the lungs, providing nourishment via inhalation.[40] British designer duo Sam Bompas and Harry Parr mixed an inhalation cocktail for the Alcoholic Architecture 2009 event in London: an alcoholic cloud of gin and tonic that visitors inhaled and consumed as they passed through the mist.[41]

Objects as constructs of sensory experiences

Every object is initially the subject of an experience, because we can only even realize its existence through our sensory impressions and their interplay with the musculoskeletal system.[42] Having said that, our sensory organs perceive differences, but not 'things' that could be distinguished as such from others:[43] "How these signals are then connected to 'objects' in no way depends only on what signals our sensory organs simply generate. On the contrary, a closer examination, [...], shows that we never use all the signals we have, but [...] select a relatively small number and supplement this selection with the recollection of perceptions stored in the memory [...] as required. This 'need' is determined in the context of the action in which we find ourselves; and this particular context never requires that we see the 'environment' as it is 'in reality' (which we cannot do in any case), but it requires only that what we perceive enables us to be successful in our actions."[44] Our sensory perceptions are therefore to be considered as "creative" actions which give rise to colors, shapes, sounds, tastes and smells within ourselves:[45] If one understands the senses not as the passive perception (of things that already exist) but as active abilities, then the perceivers only manifest or create what they perceive (for example, colors, smells, tastes) through the process of perception.[46] The theory, according to which objects are not only objects of knowledge but above all of interaction[47] not only gains credence, but also a new twist: The relationship between human and object is not only interactively completed,[48] but is thus enabled in the first place.

We can never be absolutely certain about the actual nature of an object, as "no one will ever be able to compare the perception of an object with the proposed object itself that is supposed to have brought about the perception."[49] What it is that perceived objects are "actually" composed of, and what qualities they have, lies beyond the capability of human understanding. For designers, the notion of creating objects that you do not really understand, simply because you cannot understand them, is a strange one. This means we are effectively working blindfolded and can only experience objects through the impact they have on the perceiving subjects – of which we, as designers, are ourselves one example. The discussion of the extent to which one can regard an object which can only be experienced through one's own sensory perceptions as an independent object, or regard it as a construct of one's own imagination, not only exemplifies the "realness" of the properties of things, "but also their objecthood, i.e., their oneness and their corporeal wholeness, as well as the structure of reality per se."[50]

Differences between edible and inedible objects

Most research papers on things or objects don't provide food as an example.[51] Food can be easily incorporated into many meditations about objects, e.g., papers about technical objects as well as into economic meditations on the subject of objects as commodities.[52] It appears, however, that the overarching meaning of food and its function as a social institution stand in the way of the approach of seeing food in an unbiased way as what it truly is, namely an object. In its true physical reality, food as a thing differs from other things in certain special respects – or object qualities; principally in its edibility (which is nevertheless mostly socially bestowed – see above).

How is the object "food" different from other commodities?

In the world of objects, one special physical feature about food is its edibility. Food objects are received inside the body, where they are also experienced sensorially. They are at least partly incorporated into a body; meaning they are dissolved and transformed into bodily substances. Edible objects therefore occupy a special position in the sense that one generally does not incorporate other objects and does not – at least to some extent – become physically one with them.

Another difference is that food products in a ready-to-eat (or served up) state have a short lifespan in comparison to other items. Food and drinks are consumables; i.e., they are destroyed in the course of their use. Food products are objects made to be consumed immediately; a property that food shares with other consumables such as stationery or toiletries. Unlike other consumables, however, food objects often "live" for only a brief period in their ideal "finished" state (on the plate), and their destruction immediately follows. The lifespan of ready-to-eat food products ranges from a few minutes for food served on the plate and at the right temperature (e.g., hot) to a few years for ready-to-eat long-life products such as crackers, candies, marmalade, sauerkraut or pickled vegetables, and certain beverages The purpose of (served) food is to be consumed within a certain, usually rather short period of time. Typical modes of behavior towards objects, such as collecting, owning, exhibiting or having a long-term, emotional attachment to them therefore make no sense with food or are not possible for preservation reasons. Food is perishable.[53] Preserving food products or parts of them as souvenirs or keepsakes would seem absurd. (Preserving portions of your favorite food made by your grandmother and keeping them on the sideboard as a memento would probably be considered psychologically abnormal, in spite of there being a strong emotional attachment to the object.)

Every object goes through different phases over the course of its existence: its beginning, e.g., in the form of a draft sketch, then as a model, prototype or semi-finished piece of work during the manufacturing process, and "then later being used, and finally as material that has been used up,"[54] i.e., garbage. With food products, this translates as e.g., the state of a dish as a recipe, in the form of individual ingredients, then as dough or raw mixture, after that as food ready on the plate, then in the mouth and finally either as part of the body's own substance or as bodily waste. Which of these material states are then perceived as the food in question itself, and not as raw material or garbage, depends on the mental idea we have of food. In addition to its physical presence, every object naturally also exists on the idealistic plane: as imagination, as concept, as idea. This immaterial state is especially pronounced with food because of its short-lived nature:

If we think or talk about certain food products, for example, we often have images of their (idealized) form in advertising, as a picture on the packaging, in the display cabinet or in our memories; in other words, ideational states of these everyday objects which often strongly differ from the state they are in when we actually consume them.[55]

Edible objects are destroyed during the fulfillment of their purpose – namely the act of eating: therefore, an emotional bond is only possible by association with objects that are always similar, i.e., the same kind of dish or the same food; never exactly the same, but constantly prepared anew. An edible object therefore exists not only in reality or as an idea but also as a blueprint for constant reproduction (for example as a cooking recipe, i.e., as instructions). This never-ending cycle of destruction and re-preparation which food is subject to per se describes a characteristic property of the object "food" which distinguishes it from other objects. Food is usually only in an edible condition for a short period of time before its use, which is why there is always a certain inherent process-driven quality to it.

Because of its innate purpose, food is subject to a built-in transience and impermanence, since the goal of edible objects is not only to be used but consumed (i.e., eaten). Non-transient food is a contradiction in terms. On closer inspection, however, there are two aspects to the perishability of food: one being the natural process of change or decay to which food products are subject per se due to their organic ingredients; and the other being the changes that happen due to being in a state that is physically unstable, thus causing them to be culturally interpreted as spoiled because these changes make the food seem inedible or unappealing: the soup goes cold, the wine gets warm, the sauce separates, the beer foam or whipped cream goes flat, the meat goes dry, etc.

On the other hand, trying to get around the impermanence of food products – that is, the perishability of the ingredients – is an essential driving force in the design of food and has led to the development of specific designs over the centuries. With preservation being the goal of processing and preparing food, very distinct types of taste have emerged such as the flavor of cured, pickled, candied or fermented products to name just a few.

Food as an essential object

Another special feature of food as an object is that it is essential: "Why do people need objects at all – take the basic ones, say, like chairs, sofas or cutlery? We should obviously not take the eggfryer for granted, but neither should we do so for the chair, despite it being far older. The objects we think of as plain today are still cultural inventions or linked to culture – the chair to sedentary high culture and our cutlery, especially the fork, to modern feudalism."[56] Observations like this reveal a further difference that food (and drink) has to other items: they are indispensable objects. This attribute actually sets food (and drink) apart alongside only air (or oxygen, if we also consider gases to be material objects), because even clothing, tools and housing are – depending on habitat – not necessarily essential for survival.

Food consists of "living" material

Another special feature of the object "food" is that it is exclusively created from living material: except for inorganic ingredients such as salt, extraneous life must be extinguished or acquired in order to produce food. In the process of eating, a metamorphosis is carried out from the other to the self; from the object (the food that is eaten) to the subject (the body of the eater). In the design of food, that is, during the process of "making something into food," the exact opposite happens; namely a metamorphosis from the living being to the lifeless object. In other words: With eating, a transformation takes place from the object (the food) to the subject (the person who is eating); and with designing food, a transformation from the subject (animal or plant) to the object (the food). Thus, the object "food" doubly stands at the intersection between subject and object.

While the process of eating transforms what has been eaten from object to living entity, food design – in the sense of preparing and designing food and drink – transforms a living entity into an object. Even when live seafood such as oysters, lobsters or fish are served, a symbolic transformation of the animal into a seemingly lifeless object on the plate is already done in the dressing and the serving. So food design means the transformation of living beings (animals and plants) into objects for eating and is thereby a cultural act of categorization, empowerment and acquisition. Figuratively speaking, therefore, food design is indeed a design process, and one that appropriates the environment against the background of one's own survival.

Food and its design as transformations between living beings and objects

With the exception of salt and water, all the food we eat has itself been alive[57] or is the product of living things. The nature of food preparation is also that animate beings have to be transformed into lifeless objects on the plate in a process of appropriation. Viewed in this way, food design is also a ruthless human creative process, because the design of comestibles makes food out of living beings. We have to absorb other living beings in order to eat. They are not only converted into energy inside the body and then excreted out again, but are also converted into the body's own building blocks. Adult bodies basically consist of what they have eaten and drank in the past.[58] When we eat, extraneous substances from the environment metamorphose into the body's constituent parts; this is a psychological dilemma, since we physically consist entirely of these extraneous substances, yet mentally we still maintain our own identity and subjectivity. No other object besides air, food and drink is allowed to penetrate into the interior of one's own body. Among other things, we use the specific design of the food to resolve this discrepancy between food – as an object that is both part of our environment and part of ourselves – within a short time frame. Though there are some exceptions (carrion, animal products such as honey and milk), the fact that extraneous life has to be extinguished or appropriated in order for oneself to live leads among other things to the tendency for some dishes to be designed in such a way that this link is deliberately masked.[59]

This intentional masking of raw materials can be observed in the design of various foods. One example is the deliberate destruction of a raw material's structure and the homogenization of its texture. Naturally-based foodstuffs such as meat or vegetables have fibers, cores, skeletons, skins, shells, bones or ridges. Some of the foods made from them, however, such as sausage, meatloaf, pate or puree, are totally uniform in consistency and color. A uniformly pink and soft sausage, for example, shows hardly any aesthetic similarities with its raw constituents, which consist of dead animals. Ketchup and fish sticks are also designed so that they expressly bear minimal resemblance to their main ingredients – tomato and fish respectively.[60]

Food as a design object?

Food is a material object that is physically tangible, is given a name, and has observable characteristics. To what extent are food products also design objects? According to Beat Schneider, design objects are material products of human skill and a manifestation of the human spirit: "The design of a product consists in the particular arrangement of the materials for specific human purposes, which are not determined by nature."[61]

Since artificial, i.e., man-made objects (artifacts) form the basis of art as well as of design, design science also marks the design object as distinct from art and makes a distinction between "works of art" as such and "technical works of art," or everyday objects.[62] In contrast to works of art, everyday objects can be "illustrated as part of an action" and derive "meaning only in relation to other objects."[63] Unlike art objects, design objects are always based on an idea against which the object is evaluated: "A chair's value is measured by its chairness. The elegance a chair possesses and the feeling that the chair evokes when sitting on it are the evaluation criteria."[64] In the case of food, these evaluation criteria are e.g., edibility itself, taste, oral congeniality, agreeableness, nutritiousness, etc.

Food is a commodity that is used on a daily basis and is indispensable for everyone. To what extent are these edible things that we ingest design objects as well as mere commodities?

Design objects are objects created under the influence of human activity. In this sense, foraged comestibles, such as wild fruits or nuts, are not design objects because they are not designed by people. However, the conscious categorization of an object as "edible" – i.e., its utilization, which has a specific purpose in mind – can be regarded as mankind's first infringement on nature and thus as a conscious act of design.

Food as a design object – recognition as design

If design is defined as parts of the surroundings that are shaped by mankind, this notion of design starts with the recognition and use of a foraged object. Where food is concerned, this doesn't just mean cultivation or preparation, but the selection and separation of edible natural objects from non-edible ones. Like the "objet trouvé" in art, one could regard foraged and identified food as a design object: "All art, however, begins with the objet trouvé, the ready-made, the foraged material, which inspires certain ideas in people. We are familiar with the objet trouvé from modern art and also from our own lives."[65] A cloud that looks like a horse is not created by man, but interpreted, meaning that it is imbued with meaning and can there-fore become art or design. From this perspective, the forest mush-room is also an objet trouvé which, although naturally produced, is picked and eaten by whoever finds it and infuses it with a particular meaning and a given purpose. All natural raw material undergoes a certain design process simply by being recognized as food. When a person not only sees but consciously perceives raspberries on the bush or dandelion leaves in the meadow, recognizes (interprets) them as edible, picks them and gives them a function, namely as food, and then eats them, she or he performs a deliberate action of design.[66] Of course, according to this very broad definition of the design of the surrounding environment and of food, everything that we recognize – that we name, for example – is likewise a design object. From this it follows that the entire meaningful environment, everything that has meaning to us and is consciously perceived, must be a design object.

Food is – as already mentioned – not a natural actuality, but is culturally defined. Therefore, food per se is no less than the result of a human design process, namely that which defines it as an edible object. All food is thus – at least in the broadest sense – a designed object and the result of a process of classification, preparation and/or production (food design). Since all food has a physical presence and is therefore an object, there can be no food without design; and since all food must first be recognized and defined as such, there is also none without it having been designed.

When is food designed?

Foods are socially constructed, and not natural objects as such. The boundary between "natural," foraged and "artificial," i.e., designed food cannot therefore be drawn at all, because in the broadest sense everything edible can be defined as a design object (namely when someone recognizes something as edible and uses it for their own interests, for example fruit in the jungle). Looking at it like this, there is no "natural" food whatsoever. More strictly speaking, food can be described as a design object if it is a natural product altered by humans, i.e., it is processed and pursued with a specific aim in mind. From this point of view, the deliberate growing and cultivation of plants and animals can be considered a design act, and consequently bred animals and cultivated plants can generally be considered design objects, along with agriculture and livestock products. All raw culinary materials and dishes processed or prepared by human hands are design objects in one way or another, as peeling, cutting or heating and even cooking are considered purposeful design processes.

Strictly speaking, edible design objects only emerge when these processes establish a guideline within a certain group, according to which different people are continually preparing or processing products. In this stricter sense, all food items and dishes that are continually produced according to a fixed set of rules can be called "design objects."[67] These designed objects are then reproducible and are made according to certain specifications in which the original point of the design, e.g., the idea behind a "croissant" or a "Gugelhupf" is no longer necessarily even a part of the knowledge or awareness of every person involved in the preparation. As soon as an object that falls within this category is no longer recognized only as a specific item but also as a concept or an institution and learned by convention – not just as "food" but as "pizza," "frozen peas" or "café latte," it also acts as part of a communication system in addition to its function as nourishment.[68] Such instructions include e.g., a cooking recipe that specifies the ingredients but also the shape and texture of a food, e.g., a bagel. This definition of culinary design objects includes both manually and industrially mass-produced foods.[69]

To summarize what can be said about food as a design object: Food objects form the building blocks of the human body. Food marks the interface between interior and exterior, between Other and Self. Food is a commodity and is indispensable as such. Food is defined by people and is therefore designed per se. Strictly speaking, then, food is a design object if it is deliberately altered by people; meaning grown, prepared or processed. Even more strictly speaking, food is a design object only when this design process follows predetermined rules, i.e., is conventionalized.

1   See Pudel, 2005, p. 59

2   See Barlösius, 1999, pp. 80–81

3   See Hirschfelder, 2001, p. 17; Pudel, 2005, p. 59

4   Barlösius, 1999, p. 81

5   See Lemke, 2012, p. 50

6   Lemke, 2012, p. 51

7   See Barlösius, 1999, p. 81

8   See Lemke, 2012, p. 52

9   Elschenbroich, 2010, p. 75

10   See Wiater, 2012, pp. 19–20

11   See Birus, 2000, p. 99

12   See Birus, 2000, p. 99

13   See Rützler, 2005, p. 160

14   See Wimmer, 2005, p. 36

15   See Lorenzer, 1981, pp. 13–14

16   See Lemke, 2007, p. 381

17   See Berger, Luckmann, 1989, p. 182

18   See Barlösius, 1999, p. 33

19   Barlösius, 1999, p. 93

20   Berger, Luckmann, 1966

21   See Berger, Luckmann, 1989, p. 1

22   Berger, Luckmann, 1989, p. 182

23   See Kaufmann, 2005, p. 17

24   See Mennell, 1988, p. 18

25   Berger, Luckmann, 1989, p. 182

26   See Davidson, 2006, p. 324 and Thiel, 2010, p. 11

27   See Berger, Luckmann, 1989, p. 182

28   Watzlawick, 2009, p. 94

29   Lemke, 2008, p. 218

30   See Kaufmann, 2005, p. 19

31   See Hürlimann, Reininghaus, 1996, p. 138

32   Berger, Luckmann, 1989, pp. 116–117

33   Austrian Federal Ministry for Health, Austrian Food Codex, IV. Edition, Chapter / B 14 / Meat and meat-based products; published by decree: BMGF-75210/0010- IV/B/10/2005 from 19.10.2005

34   See Rützler, 2005, p. 159

35   Foods and ingredients derived or otherwise produced from genetically modified organisms, such as rapeseed oil from genetically modified rapeseed, have not been novel food since 2004 but fall under Regulation (EC) No. 1829/2003 concerning genetically modified food and feed and Regulation (EC) No. 1830/2003 concerning the traceability and labeling of such products.

36   See Birus, 2003, p. 100

37   Elschenbroich, 2010, p. 73

38   See Glasersfeld, 2009, p. 20

39   See Kwiatkowski, 1987

40   See Guixé, 2002, p. 27

41   See Bompas, Parr, 2010, p. 152

42   See Foerster, 2009, p. 76

43   See Glasersfeld, 2009, p. 21

44   Glasersfeld, 2009, p. 22

45   See Glasersfeld, 2009, p. 29

46   See Glaserfeld, 2009, pp. 29–30

47   See Hörz, 1983

48   See Foraita, 2011, p. 54

49   Glasersfeld, 2009, p. 12

50   Glasersfeld, 2009, p. 11

51   See Elschenbroich, 2010; Baudrillard, 1968; Steffen, 1995

52   E.g., Baudrillard, 1968

53   See Korsmeyer, 2002, p. 108 and p. 145

54   See Vihma, 1997, p. 29

55   See Korsmeyer, 2002, p. 181

56   Gudrun Scholz in Steffen, 1995, p. 21

57   See Gniech, 2002, p. 8

58   To a relatively small extent, substances are also introduced into the body

via breathing, the absorption of substances through the skin, via
injections, sexual intercourse, etc.

59   See Gniech, 2002, p. 154

60   See Stummerer, Hablesreiter, 2010 (2), p. 82

61   Schneider, 2009, pp. 11–12

62   See Foraita, 2011, p. 54

63   Foraita, 2011, p. 49

64   Foraita, 2011, p. 47

65   Kubelka, 2004, p. 15

66   Understanding that the selection and definition of food is a deliberate human
        action has a strong impact on the discourse on sustainability, for example.

67   See Hablesreiter, Stummerer, 2010 (2), p. 72

68   See Barthes, 1961, p. 979 and Korsmeyer, 2002, p. 104

69   See Hablesreiter, Stummerer, 2010 (2), p. 72

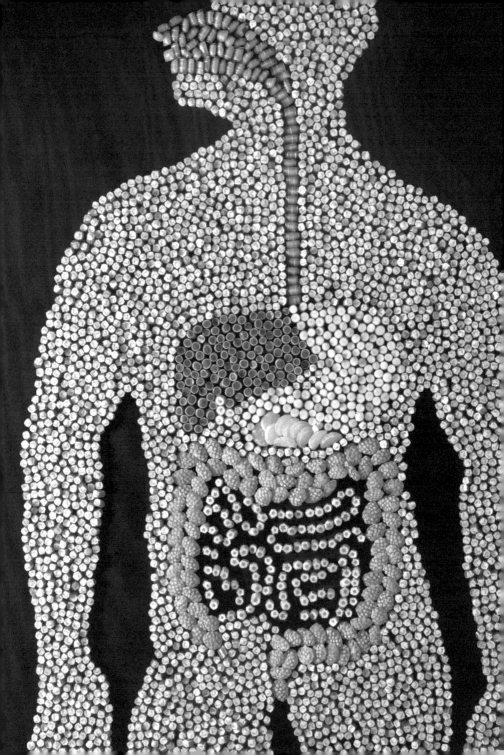

Motivations of food design

"Food design postulates new ways of relating to food."[1]

In the context of food products, design means the development and planning of food; that is, the sum of all the processes and decisions that serve in food's design. This not only concerns the visual appearance of a dish or a product, but also the design of the taste, texture, consistency, outer appearance, smell, chewing sounds and all other factors that make up the condition of the food.[2]

Food Design can be regarded as part of traditional product design, in which a conventional list of requirements can also be applied to food: Among other things, food products – as well as non-edible design objects – have to fulfill practical, aesthetic, symbolic, economic, ecological and ethical requirements. In western industrialized countries today, many foods are industrially manufactured, mass-produced goods and so no different from industrial design products such as mobile phones, pens or sunglasses: "[...] there are countless other food products – from breakfast cereals to children's sweets, pre-packed sandwiches to cooking sauces – that require the same research, development, engineering and marketing skills as does the latest Nintendo game."[3] Industrial design includes not only "traditional" design objects such as furniture, electrical appliances or vehicles but also all industrially manufactured products. From sanitary wipes to prostheses, from condoms to chewing gum, products that are seldom associated with design such as medical instruments, weapons or even industrially manufactured food are included in industrial design.

Strictly speaking, food design, as opposed to mere styling or decorating, is the result of reproducible, repeated processes that follow strict rules and have clear aims. Most cooking processes are actions that always follow a recipe, i.e., instructions, in the same way, and so mass production is not necessarily the same thing as industrial production in this sense. The sociologist Eva Barlösius also sees recipes as design concepts: "Cooking recipes are a cultural tool for guaranteeing that the dish always tastes [note: looks, smells, feels, sounds, etc.] the same as the first time, even though it is always different. The whole kitchen strives for identity through uniformity of taste [note: more precisely: through the same results for shape, color, smell, texture, sound and taste]."[4] Different kinds of pasta or pastries, such as the bagel, the pretzel or the braid, for example, were made by hand for hundreds of years yet prepared in the same way millions of times by the most diverse of people – and can therefore be quite clearly seen as design objects. In the age of industrial food processing, however, applied industrial design has resulted in a multitude of edible products. As a result, food design, like conventional design, has moved into a pivotal position between industry, manual skills, handicraft and applied art.

The causal necessity of food design

Along with the design of tools and other items for everyday use, the design of food is one of the oldest kinds of design ever. Food design is one of the primary categories of design, comparable to architecture and fashion, since the design of food and drink has to do with the way primary survival necessities are culturally implemented, as is also the case with the home environment or clothing. "In terms of human survival, food and drink are second only to the air we breathe in terms of how essential they are."[5]

The human desire to shape food in special ways and to give it meaning is causal in nature, as is the way clothing or living space are shaped or art is created. German design theorist Wolfgang Jonas sees design as the essence of being human, and the ability to design and be aware of it as an essential human quality.[6] A world without writing is conceivable, but a world without design is not, because it would mean a world without cultivated objects and without processed information. There is therefore a pressing need to design objects such as living areas, clothing, tools and food.

The history of food design

"There is a brief history and a longer history of food design. The longer history begins at the moment when instead of eating a wrapped sausage with gloved hands, it was put inside a long bun: a more efficient instrument for the task, and edible on top of that. The short history of food design begins when this type of action becomes self-reflective and is consciously integrated into the tradition of design."[7] In order to trace the beginnings of the relationship between food and design, it behooves to go further back than Martí Guixé. As mentioned above, the initial human manipulation of foraged food takes place while it is being selected and allocated as food. A first technological milestone in the history of food design appeared around 900,000 years ago: the domestication of fire, which presented people with the option of cooking.[8] Fire has therefore been in use since even before Homo sapiens emerged. This opened up completely new, hitherto undreamed of possibilities in terms of preservation, edibility and of course also taste, since certain aromas are only released through heating.[9] The consistency of the food could also be altered by heating it, which gradually caused a reduction in jaw size and freed the space necessary for the brain to grow to its current size. The British anthropologist Richard Wrangham sees cooking as the act that distinguishes humans from animals,[10] and the contrast to the consumption of raw food as the cradle of the genus homo, the race of man. The brain was only able to expand and an actual human being emerge because of the preparation of food, i.e., due to the then-novel technology of food design.[11] One of the prerequisites for the development of humans into beings that are dominant over nature with regard to the environment is thus directly linked to the design of the food.[12] "Cooking as a transition from soft to hard foods or vice versa, from hard to soft foods, proves to be a fundamental process for exploring the world."[13]

The use of fire to design food had far-reaching consequences. The available food supply increased, and cooking it also destroyed bacteria and parasites, making the food safer to eat. "The massive grinding jaw could become smaller, the mouth more suitable for articulating speech."[14]

From a food design perspective, cooking is the human creative process whose goal is the designed, edible object, namely the ready-to-eat dish. Since cooking is an active, deliberate design process with a clear aim, any kind of cooking can be viewed as a design process and the prepared meal as a design object. Preparation is thus a design process which leads to a final product – the edible object.

Ultimately, every process of preparation is a deliberate alteration and therefore a design process. Cooking is a part of this design process. In a nutshell, it can be said that: cooking is design, but conversely food design – from cultivation to serving – involves many more processes than just cooking. Design processes that have to be performed in order to obtain the desired end product in the preparation of food include peeling, slicing, seasoning, mixing, stirring, whipping, heating, cooling, kneading, tossing, pulling, drying, beating, roasting, pricking, soaking, basting, etc., all done in a certain way, sequence, time period, etc.

Motivations of Food Design

What motivates people to embellish their food in an often intricate way? When one looks at the design history of food, patterns and strategies emerge that have led on one hand to the diversification of our food and on the other to standardization – both of which continue to motivate us to constantly expand the variety of food available while at the same time setting aside certain other designs. On the question of what motivates the design of food products, three main objectives stand out: We design food to

1. increase enjoyment of the senses while eating (aesthetic function),
2. meet practical-technical aspects of all kinds (practical-technical functions), and
3. to communicate culture-specific knowledge (symbolic function).[15]

To be accepted and used, design objects – edible or not – have to meet aesthetic, practical-technical and symbolic functions. "And just as the products we design are more than tools created in response to certain physical needs, so food is required to do so much more than simply fill our bellies. In the same way that we design products for comfort, aesthetic pleasure and emotional fulfillment, so we apply design to food not just in response to our physical hunger, but also to feed our senses"[16] – and satisfy all kinds of functional needs. Applied to edible objects, this subdivision into aesthetic, practical-technical and symbolic functions corresponds with the usual evaluation of food into separate values for nutrition, enjoyment and symbolic meaning.[17] However, the practical-technical functions which foods have to meet go far beyond actual nutritional value. What is evaluated as an object's "function" and what isn't is never objective of course, but is always a question of definition, that is, a construction of meaning.[18] In everyday language, the function of an object is usually understood to be only the practical-technical applications; in design, on the other hand, the aesthetic and symbolic function is also considered.

We would like to say here that this subdivision into aesthetic, practical-technical and symbolic functions is just a tool for describing, categorizing, evaluating and analyzing objects – merely a certain point of view rather than a reflection of "absolute" reality. Even in design theory, aesthetics and function are often considered to be opposites:

"The Barricades are erected between what are really just two of the many aspects of function."[19] Ultimately, however, the relationship between the form (aesthetics) and function of an object is merely a question of the definition of the term "function." The designer James Skone, for example, defines the functions that design objects have to fulfill as follows: practical functions (technology, ergonomics, usability), aesthetic function, symbolic function, economic function, ecological function and ethical function.[20]

Aesthetic function: Taste

From a designer's point of view, food is first and foremost an object, a physical item that is perceived and has an effect on its environment. Such an object evokes certain sensory experiences, produces associations, stimulates actions, communicates knowledge, etc., i.e., it always creates responses in relation to its attributes. Its physical appearance (aesthetics) serves as a medium that communicates the perceptions associated with the object; further, it forms the essence of the object itself.

Aesthetics "as a science of sensory knowledge," as defined by the German philosopher and renaissance man Alexander Gottlieb Baumgarten in his work "Aesthetica" in 1750,[21] undoubtedly includes those sensory perceptions that are activated by food. When people aim to prepare, provide and design their food so that eating it stimulates all the senses optimally and affords the greatest possible enjoyment, they are also looking to stimulate their minds, thereby heightening sensory awareness. Since the dawn of human history, people have invested far more creativity and time in intensifying the experience of eating than a purely pragmatic world view could ever justify. Wafer-thin chocolate biscuits, multi-layered, liquid-filled, crunchily coated and praline-rolled chocolates, light and airy sorbets, fluffy creams or baked goods rolled or layered out of thin pastries show that using food to orchestrate the senses is one of Food Design's major driving forces.[22]

Among an object's aesthetic features include its shape, color, material or surface. "They are the 'signs' that make a commodity 'legible' and give visual clues to its use."[23] Interestingly, the aesthetics of most everyday commodities are primarily perceived visually, while the

aesthetic impressions of food are primarily gustatory (i.e., relating to the sense of taste). Basically, aesthetics encompasses all sensory perceptions that an object can evoke (e.g., taste, smell, or sound). "If the user doesn't like one of these signals, even a very practical commodity has little chance."[24] In the case of food, its aesthetic features are e.g. its taste, its smell, its texture or the chewing sound it makes. They also give clues about the practical value
 of the food, e.g. the noise made by breaking or biting into food suggests its nutritional value: while a chocolate bar sounds dull when broken (and contains a lot of sugar), a rice cracker (which contains hardly any calories) sounds very light.[25]

Simply put, one could describe taste as the aesthetic of edible objects. The term "taste" is ambiguous, however: "The English term "taste" has had several meanings in its history, all of which relate in some way to the idea of intimate acquaintance with an object by means of one's own sensory experience. Precursor terms include usages that mean to touch, to smell, and to test."[26] On the one hand 'taste' is understood to be a property an object possesses and on the other, it refers to the sensation of taste being one of the five senses (the gustatory sensory perception); and thirdly it means the ability to distinguish "good" from "bad"[27] – or the verdict on a taste.

"Taste" is a key word in both food and design, however either subject uses it quite differently: The taste of a dish is normally understood to refer to the gustatory sensory perception, whereas the question of taste in design objects means the opinion of the beholder, namely whether or not he or she likes it.

Scientific taste

Scientifically speaking, taste is both an object property and the sensory perception of it. The perception of taste actually only takes place on the tongue to a small extent. Taste cells are distributed throughout the entire mouth cavity, so they can also be found on the palate, in the larynx and in the esophagus. These "taste cells" are arranged in groups of 15 to 40 as so-called taste buds. Newborns are born with about 10,000 taste cells, and their numbers gradually reduce to just over 2,000 in old age.[28]

The physiological taste is the sensation of taste experienced around the mouth and throat, but it is only a small part of the actual sensation of eating. Today, scientists consider there to be five fundamental senses of taste: sweet, sour, salty, bitter and umami. The word "umami" comes from Japanese and refers to the sensory impression given by glutamate, which can best be described in English as "full-bodied," "spicy" or "piquant." As an additive flavor enhancer, glutamate is now registered under the number E 62. In addition to the five basic tastes, the sensors also distinguish the taste qualities "astringent" and "pungent" as a stimulation of the trigeminal cranial nerve through pain-inducing molecules in pepper, paprika, chili and ginger. In practice, the five primary tastes barely exist in their pure form – for example, only table salt tastes truly salty – most foods are perceived as a combination of several basic tastes.[29]

From a scientific point of view, the sense of taste has developed in order to ensure human survival. "Sweet" signifies a high carbohydrate content and thus a high nutritional value; "umami" suggests good sources of protein. Salty is important for ionic balance, sour is good for digestion. "Bitter" includes a warning feature to protect us from consuming inedible or poisonous food.[30]

The product feature or sensory perception commonly referred to as "taste" is quite different to the purely physiological taste, i.e., the sensation of the five basic tastes and combinations thereof; a complex interplay of the perceptions of all five senses.[31] Because if something "tastes good," it usually means that it looks good, feels good in the mouth, sounds good when chewed, smells good, and so on.

The tongue and nose – a perfect team

The gustatory and the olfactory system – that is, the sense of taste and smell combine when we eat. They have the job of converting smell and taste stimuli into impulses which are then transmitted to the brain. The most important organ for taste perception is not the mouth, but the nose.[32] First it delivers a remote analysis of what is being served up, establishing among other things how fresh it is, what aromas it contains and how it might taste. The nose as well as the eye first checks from a distance whether something is ripe, edible or has gone off.

Even after the food has been found to be good and put in the mouth, the "taste" of a food is mainly perceived through the "retronasal smell", so via food molecules that reach from the throat through the posterior nostrils to the smell receptors of the nose. There, special receptor proteins respond to the chemical interactions of smells and tastes and can thereby identify up to 10,000 different aromas. Only the nose's perceptions can differentiate between all the nuances that the five main tastes contain. So, with your nose shut, you can tell that something tastes sweet, but not whether it tastes of strawberry, cherry or mango. We only experience the complex flavors of food when the specific aroma particles reach the receptors of our nose. With a blocked-up nose, you can hardly taste anything.[33]

The mouth is therefore a rather poor taste organ, but as a tactile organ it still plays a central role in perceiving the object properties of what we are eating. The tongue "feels" the food and transmits the corresponding stimuli to the brain. Processes such as chewing, sucking, palpating and mashing the food effectively influence the sense of eating by warming up what is being eaten and by evaporating volatile molecules that are then smelled. Texture and consistency are therefore central design factors with food.

The cultural relativity of taste

Though nature demands that people eat, it does not dictate what they like and what they don't. The function of taste as a warning system against the consumption of harmful or toxic substances is scientifically disputed. For one thing, the fact that many extremely toxic substances taste "good" or have no taste at all suggests that this is not the case. For example, several highly toxic metal salts taste sweet (e.g., lead, cadmium, or titanium compounds in paints). On the other hand, a tolerance for bitter tastes can be developed in the case of caffeine or nicotine or with painful tastes such as chili.[34] More highly developed animals have the ability to learn about their food. These learning processes can then override biological impulses.[35]

Every society sets restrictions on the natural compulsion to eat with an extremely complex system of rules and conventions that state how food intake should be set. These restrictions include the selection of basic ingredients, how they are put together, the manner and length of preparation, location, technique, utensils, etc. involved in eating as well as defining food rituals and food taboos. The culturally learned taste – "taste" in the third sense of the word, the judgment of taste – serves to legitimize this socially established classification system. The background to conventions and restrictions on food intake has been debated a great deal in sociology and other subjects, in most the cases proving that these rules are not physical-biological, but have social, mythological or cultural bases.

From a physiological point of view, there is no reason why people in Europe do not eat dogs or cats. However, there is very likely a cultural reason why people, for example in Central Europe, don't like to eat these animals: because they are culturally classified as "inedible" and are therefore eschewed under the pretext of their physiological taste, when it is in fact a cultural issue.

Taste is therefore always relative, not only due to individual differences in sensory perception, but above all because of the –

mostly subconscious – classifications of these sensory stimuli. Every person, every society, every culture tastes things differently. "There is no such thing as a universal, global language of food. We comprehend food exclusively with our mental dialects via taste and sensory perceptions."[36] What is eaten is not primarily determined via instinct, but is predominantly culturally installed. There is no universal formula that can combine the five basic tastes to make a tasty meal or a successful food product. What tastes good depends on the culinary tradition in question and varies enormously from group to group: "food practices and attendant taste preferences exhibit strikingly different patterns in different societies."[37] Even physiologically unpleasant taste sensations such as bitter coffee or spicy chili, can be culturally used in a positive way and thus be popular with large sections of the population.[38] It is no coincidence that smell and taste codes are a field of research in semiotics,[39] and that semiotics has now become an integral part of taste research.

Taste is therefore not necessarily a question of impartial enjoyment, but also a social instrument for legitimizing a certain order. Consequently, taste also functions as a method of imparting identity, as a storehouse of traditional behavioral patterns or of a traditional receptacle of knowledge, as a carrier of ideology and as a means of social differentiation, as for example French sociologist Pierre Bourdieu described in detail in his book "La Distinction, Critique sociale du jugement" (Distinction, A Social Critique of the Judgment of Taste" (1979). With these functions of taste, there is no difference between "the taste of food" and cultural or artistic taste.[40] The taste of food, as well as other kinds of taste (e.g., musical taste, taste in fashion, artistic taste), has a cultural flavor, especially in its functions as a distinguishing feature and a method of differentiation. If Swiss social anthropologist Andreas Wimmer describes "culture" as a continuous process of negotiating meaning, in which people "relate to each other, leading to the forming of compromises for the purpose of social closure and its corresponding cultural segregation"[41] then the taste of food is a means of accomplishing such segregation.

Taste research / food sensors

The relativity of taste is a major problem for food producers – yet it is a stylistic device for food designers. Taste research, usually on behalf of the food industry, tries to scientifically measure the range of sensory perceptions experienced while eating. An important foundation for taste research is the sensory evaluation of food.

In order to "measure" taste and convert it into scientific data, methods of chemically analyzing the food in question are usually compared with the evaluations of sensory test persons (tasters). An example of such a test is the optimization of foods that stand out acoustically like cornflakes, snack foods or sausages, which – if they are produced in a sufficiently large number – are also tested with regard to the noise they cause. With a so-called Acoustic Analyzer, the chewing sound of a food can be emulated and recorded. The results can then be collated with customer requests and optimized. Usually, a suitable "target sound" is initially determined for a particular marketing concept. Then the properties of the food object, such as composition, baking time, geometry, etc., are variegated until the food causes the correct target sound upon eating.[42]

Depending on the focus of the test, "normal citizens" from the street (hedonic approach) or sensory-trained experts (analytical method) can be used. The claim to generate data that is not based on the more-or-less subjective feedback of test persons has in recent years increasingly led to the use of measurement techniques that represent subconscious reactions, such as the measurement of heart rate, pupil movement, the recording of facial expressions, changes in skin tone and suchlike.

The attempt to find generally valid, scientific evaluation criteria for physiological taste, however, is condemned to failure from the outset for the reasons mentioned above. In the same way as it is not possible to scientifically analyze a work of art by looking at the proportions of different colors and color frequencies on the surface of a canvas and then draw conclusions about how to create a different, new painting that appeals to as many people as possible, physiological taste cannot be rigorously described scientifically. Neither food taste nor artistic taste are simply about absolute – that is, scientifically measurable – distinguishing criteria (like the chemical composition of the ingredients and suchlike), but about the processing of these sensations in the brain. This processing can only be performed by means of the human "measuring device" and is therefore never absolute, but dependent on experience, education, culture etc.[43]

Aesthetic taste

Taste is not exactly an object-property per se (or a synergy of it) but an association – or an evaluation – of these properties, in which this evaluation can be of a political or moral nature, or a general expression of a certain way of thinking (see Grimm, 1984).

Absolute ("good") taste itself does not exist, but is socially acquired, since taste is an individual or cultural construct – namely the subjective, situational, social, etc. evaluation of an object's properties (or the sensory stimuli that they evoke) within the boundaries of one's own culture. With eating, both variations of taste – the gustatory and the aesthetic – meet, but at the same time they are never perceptible or conceivable independently of each other. The characteristic taste of a product can be chemically captured in the form of the substances involved, however this "synthetic" taste is never the same as the actual taste sensation itself because it only registers with the transmission of sensory stimuli in the brain and therefore bear no relationship to the social, cultural, true-to-life etc. connotations. The aesthetic features are therefore always emotional, subjective and culture-dependent and can never be named and evaluated precisely.[44]

One example of the situational evaluation of tastes is e.g., the effect of neophobia, or the intuitive rejection of new, unusual tastes.

In a test involving cocoa and milk drinks one of the most popular flavors of all time, vanilla, was surprisingly classified as bitter, i.e., negatively rated because it was served in an unusual mix, in plain milk instead of cocoa.[45] This test shows that vanilla does not taste "good" or "sweet" per se, and can under certain circumstances also be perceived as "bitter," i.e., "bad."

When food is tasted, the incoming sensory stimuli are categorized, i.e., the significant is separated from the non-significant. This act of separation happens from a particular perspective.[46] According to American philosopher Susanne Langer's symbol theory, the process of sensory experience is already a formulation. Certain predominant themes (Susanne Langer refers to them as "forms") have to be chosen out of the disorganized hotchpotch of sensory stimuli that we perceive in order for anything to be recognized from the chaos of sensory data.[47] Looked at in this way, one could consider perception itself – even that of food – as a form of design.[48] The ability to see, smell or taste things instead of just receiving sensory impressions of them happens by immediately and unconsciously abstracting a form from every sensory experience, which we then use to classify it and to grasp and comprehend it as a whole, as a "thing." According to Susanne Langer, perception is something active rather than a purely passive input/receiving of data, a process of formation that takes place by means of the sensory organs, the nervous system and the brain. Perception is an abstraction; exactly how it happens already allows the way of understanding that which is perceived.[49]

The sensation that we commonly refer to as the taste of a meal comes about as a result of chemical, electrical, and neurological processes that are categorized and processed emotionally and cognitively in the brain.[50] This cognitive processing chain has not yet been researched and it is questionable whether it can be scientifically recorded at all. Taste emerges at the interface between the interior world and the exterior world. It is therefore not a physically measurable entity, and not (pure) instinct, but is above all a mental construct.

Thus, like all other sensory perceptions, taste is not an absolute, predictable brain response to external chemical and physical stimuli, but a processing and interpretation of such that gives rise to its perception in the brain. The taste of food can therefore be designed not only on the physical level of its ingredients, but also on the cognitive level of perception. All factors along the reaction chain – from the first stimulus to the emotional-cognitive classification in the brain – influence what we then perceive as "taste."[51] Taste can therefore be designed into the cognitive and emotional context of meaning at the level of the stimulus molecules, the stimulus reception and signal formation, the signal transmission and signal categorization (e.g., through other sensory or physical, emotional or cognitive influences).[52] Factors that have an influence on the experience of taste, either by chance or in the form of active interventions, are possible for example through one of the other four senses. The influence of smells, sounds, light, etc. on taste has already been empirically tested and confirmed. Furthermore, taste is co-designed from emotions, moods, expectations, memory, experience, distraction, etc., as test results cannot always be explained from the chemical-physical properties of the ingredients. For instance, one tool of cognitive influence is disgust as a control mechanism for culturally learned taste: Vegetarians may feel sickened by the smell of meat; religious groups may be sickened at the sight of ingredients that are forbidden according to their beliefs; etc.

Taste is not just a sensory perception, it is also a social practice (an institution) for helping to make everyday decisions ("what am I eating?"), as well as a kind of learned communication structure that provides behavioral guidance within a group. Taste can be converted into a symbol and, as such, instrumentalized in order to transport concepts far away from the sphere of nutrition and call for certain socially expected behavior. In this respect, the "taste of food" doesn't differ from art, fashion or music taste, because there is also a "taste in aromas," a "taste in sounds" etc.

Taste as a cultural construct / taste is open to interpretation

The perception of gustatory taste in fact happens not on the tongue and palate, but in the head. The French literary scholar Roland Barthes equated taste with concepts:[53] "Eating a rare steak is thus both a natural and a spiritual act."[54] This means that any kind of intellectual development can also alter taste. Most children, for example, instinctively avoid eating bitter or spicy foods such as coffee, beer, chilli, or red mould cheese, whereas many adults like to eat them following adequate "training."[55] Taste can also be learned: one reason, why the evaluation of products based on chemical analysis seems to make only limited sense, whereas it emphasizes the importance of symbolic meanings in food products. Food products have to be designed in such a way that they can also be interpreted and accepted by specific users in a given cultural context – a task that is usually achieved subconsciously through intuition and experience when new food items are developed. To achieve this, knowledge of the cultural context in question is an indispensable requirement. The result is then usually optimized through trial and error based on the outcomes of surveys. However, this approach involves the problem that only knowledge that one is aware of can be assessed by means of surveys, whereas subconscious associations and preferences often only appear in the sales figures.

The system of cognitively classifying chemical and physical flavor stimuli is so complex that an empirical study of taste involving its entire context (from the physical condition of the body through emotions and environmental influences to cognition and socio-culturally learned things)[56] seems to be practically unfeasible. This means that how taste works is not really researched; perhaps it can't be, and – at least at this time – it is not a question of empirical evidence, but of how it is viewed. Taste is not an objective sensation, neither is it an objectively describable object property, but it is a mechanism that justifies patterns of behavior – and in its negative form, disgust, a tool that guarantees adherence to and survival of these patterns of behavior. Accordingly, taste – just like disgust – is a mechanism for putting into practice the respectively determined categorization of the environment into "edible" and "inedible," and to legitimize and be able to rationalize it. The boundary between taste and disgust is a blurred one; within this gray area changes take place in the culturally prescribed patterns of behavior concerning food. Through transgressions – whether from provocation, decadence, xenophilia or out of necessity – a group's food register or food behavior changes over time. Taste and disgust act as the guardians of previously set codes of conduct or manners ("morals"), because they are – with a few exceptions, such as food that is decaying – rationally incomprehensible, yet purely emotional, and therefore sacrosanct, because they cannot be dismissed by rational argument. There are no factual reasons why something tastes "good" or "bad." In that sense, taste is in certain ways absolute, because whoever doesn't respect taste and disgust is threatened with exclusion from the group. Taste could therefore also be seen as an instrument of power that serves the cohesion of the group.

Taste as a bonus

As an object property of food, aesthetic taste has no practical value in any case; but it is a bonus that is not entirely necessary in order to perform the function of edible objects. The practical value of food is to keep the body alive, but food that has no taste or tastes bad is also nourishing – as long as it has some nutritional value and isn't poisonous. Tastiness is therefore the aesthetic quality of a dish, a meal or a drink – whether it is experienced visually, gustatorily or on another sensory level – and has experiential value, which is nevertheless considered of central importance when eating. If one for example were to color a tomato soup blue, it would not change its nutritional value, but the experiential value or enjoyment would change a lot. It is open to debate whether this changes the actual taste. The "objectively measurable" taste (for example, blindfolded) would remain the same, but the subjectively experienced taste would be entirely different.

Another example of how aesthetics (in this case the form) has a lasting effect on the taste of a material is cotton candy (candyfloss). It was invented in 1897 by confectioners William Morrison and John C. Wharton of Nashville, Tennessee, and presented at the 1904 World's Fair in St. Louis. To make this, sugar is heated to its melting point of about 150 degrees Celsius and pressed through tiny holes in a centrifuge. It then congeals in cold air into gossamer threads which form its rough structure. The end product is not crystalline like sugar, but amorphous and soft like cotton wool. This different (technical) design of the selfsame material (sugar) completely changes the perception of its taste. The airy-light, foamy and at the same time rough texture - which congeals back into lumps after a few hours – causes a totally different sensory experience on the tongue and palate than the sucking of a sugar cube in spite of the ingredients being the same.[57]

In a similar fashion to works of art, the boundary between practical and exchange value or surplus value[58] in everyday use also becomes blurred with food products, as the taste – i.e., the sensory perception of the food object – is understood to be a central part of the practical value – what it indeed is in the sense of cultural taste. For most food products, the aesthetic aspect is an essential feature. Upon changing it, the object is perceived as another, even if the technical function does not change. The interpretation of the aesthetic aspect as part of the use value (i.e., as a practical-technical feature) is an essential distinguishing feature that food has over other commodities. In the way their basic functions are interpreted, food products are rather to be considered works of art among the range of design objects. If the aesthetic surplus value of an edible object lies in its taste and thus in the pleasure of eating it, then it is quite comparable with the surplus value of an inedible object, which lies in the pleasure of owning it.[59]

A further example of the strong emphasis on aesthetics in food products is the different shapes available in Italian pasta, made from nothing more than water and durum wheat semolina. Its use value (nutritional value) is always the same. However, depending on whether it is smooth or rippled, thick or thin, long or short, straight or curved, etc., or has cavities into which one can feel with the tongue, it tastes very different. The variation in shape has yet another effect on the taste: depending on the shape and surface of the pasta (the latter depends among other things on whether the dough is pressed by bronze or Teflon dies), it sticks to the sauce differently. For example, the amount of sauce (depending on its consistency), which sticks to the noodles and thus the taste impression varies according to the mix ratio of pasta to sauce[60] – this effect could already be considered a practical-technical function. The taste not only depends on the ingredients (contents), but also on the technical design (form, texture, etc.) of the same.

Practical-technical functions

For food to be eaten, not only does it have to "taste," it has to do its job too. Just like other commodities, food fulfills various technical functions. The main function of food is to nourish the body: Food products must first and foremost be suitable for consumption. In addition to its basic function of keeping us alive, food has to meet a wide range of other practically oriented needs, such as: be durable, easy to prepare, stackable, bite-sized or transportable. Food is deliberately designed so that it spoils as slowly as possible, does not dry out, can be broken into equal pieces easily and without getting dirty, or is easy to eat without cutlery. People prefer, e.g., food that they can bite off easily or that they can carry well.
The fulfillment of all sorts of purpose-oriented functions – as in the case of non-edible objects – forms a central task of design and consistently influences the shape of the finished product. "The specific

shapes of many food products result directly from their function. Food is supposed to be a pleasure to the eye and palate, but we also design it according to criteria and are even willing to forego nuances of taste in return."[61] A simple example of this is foods that have a specific purpose, such as ready meals, canned goods or fast food.

Another example of how technical functions can influence design is the transportability of bread. Of course, a transport-friendly design initially depends on the chosen means of transport. Bread before motorization was made suitable for transport by forming it into ring loaves such as bagels, pretzels or simits. Tied together with a string or threaded onto sticks, bread with holes can be stored and carried easily from A to B. A person can carry 10, 20, 30 or more pretzels or bagels threaded onto a string in one hand, without the need for extra containers such as bags or boxes. "The finished bagels were threaded five dozen to a string and hung on the door handles of the shops."[62]

The "function" of an object is commonly understood to mean the practical-technical function. Since design theory also considers sensory attributes such as appearance or taste to be functions of an object (aesthetic function), the "practical-technical functions" is what is referred to in design with regard to the proper fulfillment of an object's (predefined) purpose: In common usage, 'functional' refers to practical-technical functions. These are rational and relatively simple to name and evaluate accurately. Practical-technical functions are object characteristics that facilitate or improve the usability of the object, such as manageability, durability, reliability, safety, technical quality, ergonomics and ecological value.[63]

In cuisine, the practical-technical function of "manageability" can be found for example in the form of pre-portioning. For example, until the middle of the nineteenth century sugar was usually traded in sugar loaves.[64] These weighed up to fifty kilograms and had to be painstakingly shredded at home with appropriately sharp tools. It is true that pre-portioned sugars such as "perled sugar" or "almond sugar" were known in some places as early as the 15th century. The modern sugar cube, however, was first developed by the Moravian sugar manufacturer Jakub Kryštof Rad in present-day Dačice after 1840 and marketed in 1843 under the name "Theewürfel" (tea cube) or "Wiener Würfel" (Viennese cube).[65]

The practical-technical functions of food include among other things efficiency of cultivation, harvesting and processing, ideal suitability for packaging, consumption and transportability, portionability, suitability as a take-away, digestibility and health-promoting qualities through to functional food.[66]

One good example of how functional demands affect the design of food products is sacramental bread. Firstly, it is surprising that this ritual bread is not reminiscent of either bread or a human body (the body of Christ) in its design. Instead, the almost colorless, tasteless, round wafer is primarily functionally determined with regard to its shape – apart from the symbolism of the round form. It is straightforward, i.e., it is made with minimal use of raw materials and is therefore economical (the round shape, however, causes a lot to be wasted). The actual use value in terms of calorie content is practically zero. It is extremely non-perishable, pre-portioned and bite-sized, which makes it easier to handle and distribute around the church, as the priest doesn't have to break the "bread." Larger wafers usually have a notch running across them which ensures a simple, fast and neat divide without using utensils.

Most of the practical aspects specified for conventional, i.e., non-edible design, also apply to the design of food. The terminology sometimes differs, though: where people talking about ergonomics and comfort with furniture, with food these functions are described in terms of palatability, mouthfeel and digestibility. Ergonomics plays an important role not only in the design of seating furniture and the like, but also in food. It is no coincidence that chocolates and sweets are round and thus, especially when sucked on, they are well-suited to the human eating apparatus of the tongue, palate, etc. In turn, food seldom has triangular or sharp-edged shapes. Instead, meat, fish or chocolate are preferred in rounded, elongated shapes that can be held easily in the hand and which one can easily take a bite from: Sausages, fish fingers, chocolate bars, etc. owe their shape to their adaptation to the human body, among other things.

What works?

What improves the utilization of an object – in this case, the edibility of food – and what doesn't depends on the point of view, i.e. it is relative. "The practical function of objects is [...] also a cultural invention safeguarded by social convention."[67] Which specific properties serve to facilitate usability depends on the point of view or the system of thought within which one operates. Even those object properties that are considered functions are more culturally predetermined than absolute and therefore also change with the spirit of the times. For Erlhoff and Marshall, function is what an action aims for. Function is therefore a consequence of a previously existing aim, i.e., an abstract train of thought against the backdrop of the actual action. It is not a constant, "but a variable that depends on the approach and application by the user."[68]

The relativity of the functions required can be according to ideological context, e.g., the need for sacramental bread to be "crumb-free," having contributed decisively to the paper-thin wafers establishing themselves over the consumption of real bread in Catholic observances. "At that time [note: Council of Florence, 1439] the sacramental wafer was already unrivaled as the communion bread of the Western Church. Its character is very much in keeping with the Catholic conception of the Eucharist."[69] The non-perishability, pre-portioning and dividing groove of the wafer also fulfill a function that is religiously motivated. As the Christian doctrine of transubstantiation, which was elevated to a dogma at the 4th Lateran Council in 1215, assumes that in the process of transformation, bread and wine actually and objectively "transubstantiate" into the body of Jesus,[70] the sacramental wafer is to be specially treated as the "real," corporeal Jesus: "If one perceives Christ to be present in the consecrated bread, it is obvious that no crumb of it should fall to the ground where it could be trampled on, and that the bread should not go moldy or otherwise be spoiled if it were to be kept longer – it would be happening to Christ himself."[71] Such practical considerations even go as far as the question of whether Jesus suffers in the chewing,[72] which is again reflected – consciously or coincidentally – in the design: the wafer is so thin that it melts on the tongue and can be swallowed whole.

The relevance of practical functions

Even in early theoretical reflections on architecture and design, e.g., in the work of the Roman architect and author Marcus Vitruvius Pollio (80–10 B.C.), "De architectura libri decem" (Ten Books on Architecture), which is central to Western architectural culture, practical-technical functions are highly valued. Vitruvius defines the three main pillars of architecture as firmitas (stability), utilitas (functionality) and venustas (aesthetics).[73] According to these, a building or a designed object must chiefly fulfill practical-technical functions: it should be stable, technically perfect and functional – and only then be beautiful as well.[74] To this day, in Western European culture everyday objects should serve people, be it as an instrument, tool or practical object of everyday use.[75] It is only practical-technical functions that legitimize a commodity's existence. "While the function gives the object 'reason,' so to speak, and thereby justifies its existence, the essence of the object is embodied in its form."[76]
However, this differs from the object "food," for which the priorities are usually the other way around. In contrast to most other design objects, in the case of food products it is the technical-functional properties that take a back seat, as opposed to the aesthetic ones.

With food, the practical and technical aspects have to be of a lower priority than the sensory experience (taste), which is in the fore-ground – at least on the conscious level of evaluation, which is also verbally communicated. While a meal should be "tasty" rather than durable, efficiently produced or stackable first and foremost, appliances, furniture, cars or buildings – at least when it comes to the rational justification of their practical value – should primarily function properly and only then be pleasing to the senses: A car (at least officially) is used not because it is blue, but because it is fast. Noodles on the other hand are not eaten because they are prepackaged, extremely non-perishable and quick to prepare and eat, but because they are "tasty."

A clear distinction in dealing with edible objects compared to other design objects is the emphasis on aesthetics rather than on the technical functions. Food is legitimized primarily through its taste (aesthetic function), while other everyday objects are legitimized through their practical-technical functions. Any violation of this convention is perceived as immoral (e.g., the production of food for profit above all other considerations) or unhealthy (e.g., ready meals, fast food) or, conversely, as over-sentimental or irrational, such as when someone buys an old radio that barely works. This kind of social custom lifts food from the pragmatic manner in which other commodities are dealt with on the conscious decision-making level and places it into a sphere of the irrational and emotional – in a way that is otherwise only accepted in works of art, collector's items or representational objects. Subconsciously, however, the evaluation of sensory attributes with practical ones is not so straightforward either in edible or non-edible objects. Cars are also bought for aesthetic reasons, for example for their sporty from or for making the right kind of engine noise. Likewise, Biedermeier chairs are considered "good" furniture, even though they hardly fulfill their function as seats with great distinction.

Functionalism

The tradition of placing a high value on functions that are rational and comprehensible has survived to this day in architecture and in the design of non-edibles. The appreciation of practical-technical functions no doubt also has something to do with the fact that they are easier to communicate verbally than sensory aspects, and are thought of as rationally justifiable object property irrespective of individual "liking." Purpose alignment found its zenith in functionalism and neo-functionalism (especially at the Ulm School of Design), which made the axiom "form follows function" its guiding principle.[77] The phrase "form follows function" dates back to the journal article by American architect Louis Henry Sullivan (1856–1924) – "The Tall Office Building Artistically Considered" (1896).[78] According to Papanek, the expression "form follows function" had already been coined in 1739 by the American sculptor Horatio Greenough.[79] Functionalism attempted to develop the form (aesthetics) of a designed object (exclusively) from its function. "Form follows function" was initially opposed to aesthetization and ornamentation, as it elevated the practical-technical functions of an object to its characteristic, stylistic element. The concept became one of the defining principles of modern 20th century architecture, inspiring the German Werkbund and later the Bauhaus and the Ulm School of Design.[80] Basically, functionalism is a method of optimizing practical value, though from a functionalist perspective this refers only to the practical value for the user. The essential criteria for a "good" form are born of practicality, economic efficiency and safety.[81] Interestingly enough, these very criteria are rather negatively viewed today – with the exception of safety in relation to "good" food.

What would functionalistic food be?

Applied to food and drink, the ideals of functionalism seem absurd. What kind of design could possibly reflect food's innate function to provide the body with nutrients? Which "good" form suggests itself from fat or protein content? One could perhaps call the natural forms in which nutrients occur in ingredients their very own form. It would then follow that "good" form would ultimately amount to a rejection of human design and of design itself. Another possible interpretation of "good" form for food products would be aesthetic clues to ingredients and their effects: e.g., red as a design feature to indicate that something is sweet and contains carbohydrates, or different intensities of yellow to indicate the fat content of cheese. Cheese is in fact colored with carotene to make it look richer and tastier. However, it is for precisely this kind of design ideology that the food industry is so heavily criticized.

From a functionalist perspective, one would have to consider – for example – the wide range of Italian pasta shapes that are available as an aestheticized affectation and not intended for practicality, because having only one single type of pasta would do what pasta is supposed to do equally well – i.e., fill you up – and most importantly, it would do so significantly more efficiently with regard to production, distribution, storage, preparation, composition etc. Many traditional foods – e.g., various pasties and pastries – are very decorative. If one were to consistently apply the principles of functionalism, the design of food products would be reduced to their sole purpose of keeping the body alive. Functionalistic food could then imply for example nutrition pills as they have been portrayed in science fiction films and other visions of the future, or nutrient solutions which perfectly fulfill their purpose in every respect via drip bags.

In stark contrast to food as it occurs in nature, a meal, which prioritizes the fulfillment of practical-technical functions as opposed to aesthetics i.e., taste, could however also be described as functionalistic food. Functional food such as fast food, ready meals and processed food generally tend to be viewed negatively in public debates, however, unlike functional architecture or functional product design. In this respect, there is a big difference between edible design objects and non-edible ones. A food product design that values functional criteria above aesthetics goes against social conventions. Even in western industrialized nations, food is still considered as pre-industrial craftsmanship, meaning its quality is demonstrated above all by aesthetic values and tradition.

Indicating functions

One special kind of practical-technical function is the so-called "indicating functions," a term coined in the 1970s at Offenbach University of Art and Design in Germany.[82] Indicating functions are described as the ability (quality, property) of an object to communicate the (intended) mode of operation to the user by means of its design. Theoretically, the term is based on Susanne Langer's text "Philosophy in a New Key,"[83] in which she separates the concept of signs into indications and symbols. "Indications" in the sense of the indicating functions are those signals by means of which an object directly and instantly communicates its technical functions. Specifically, this refers to design features that indicate certain functions or modes of use. This can be done graphically-visually (e.g., with markings or arrows) or by styling or coloring, choice of material etc. For example, cylinders indicate the option of rotating or pressing; oblong recesses the option of shifting, slotting or sliding; visible joints, hinges and suchlike the option of folding, etc. Of course, the vocabulary used always has to be rooted in cultural terms to be understandable.[84]

Indicating functions are intended to convey the manner in which an object functions through the object itself, that is to say to provide a kind of instruction manual contained in the design itself. A red switch, for example, indicates that it can be pressed or flipped, in so doing setting off a process that is essential for its operation. Some of these guidelines come from ergonomics, like grasping a handle. Others have a cultural origin: while a stool or a chair could actually be used in a variety of ways, we have socially learned to place our buttocks on the horizontal platform while keeping the thighs at right angles to the lower legs and upper body. Even the ability to interpret the symbolism of a red button correctly requires a certain cultural grounding.[85]

With food products, color for example is used as an indicating function: Sweets, puddings, ice creams, juices and yogurts are e.g., pinkish as an indication of having a raspberry or strawberry flavor; yellow as an indication of lemon or vanilla flavor. Because these color codes are based on culture-specific knowledge, the association of taste with color can differ considerably in other parts of the world. While Europeans have learned to expect sweet foods that are pink or red to have a strawberry flavor, Japanese people associate this color with the taste of plums.

Handles, switches, levers, etc. are also technical indicators that invite a particular type of action. "Indicators therefore convey two things: On the one hand, the so-called essential features indicate what kind of product it is; by a certain number and selection of indicators in a specific configuration, we can work out that "this is a mobile phone," "a remote control" or "a calculator."[86] With food, this categorization is usually less about function than about the material, because the categorization of food is often down to the main ingredient: Bread and pastries, meat dishes, salad, confectionery, etc. Other essential characteristics of food that communicate what type of food it is include texture, taste, temperature or how it is arranged on the plate.

Examples of object properties that communicate the type of culinary object:

Object attribute   hot + liquid/viscous = soup
Object attribute   cold + liquid = drink
Object attribute   sweet + solid = pudding
Object attribute   sweet + creamy = mousse
Object attribute   savory + creamy = spread; etc.

"On the other hand, the indicating functions signal the practical functions of a product; they mediate between human and technology, explain the product and enable easy, smooth-running use."[87] Food products also give clues about how they should be used. The grooves on the upper side of a chocolate bar indicate that you don't have to bite to get a small piece of chocolate, but that the slab can instead be easily and effortlessly broken into approximately equal units along these predetermined breaking points without making a lot of crumbs. The same applies to baked goods with predefined dividing grooves such as the Viennese Kaisersemmel (Kaiser roll) or the Turkish "Çiçek Ekmeği" (flower bread).

Another indicating function is the matching geometry and size of the processed cheese or ham slice and the toasting bread slice. The square shape, which is actually unnatural for ham and cheese, shows that these slices are intended as a topping for toasted bread and wordlessly suggests how to put the individual components together to make a ham and cheese toasty.

The indicating functions as a user manual

When we perceive a shape, we automatically associate certain behaviors to it based on our experience base. This applies to food as well as furniture or clothing. The fact that objects elicit a certain behavior or imply a certain use can also be the case with edible objects. Just as a chair as an object elicits a certain, culturally developed posture,[88] ergonomics also plays a role in food products when it comes to showing how an object is to be used: elongated edible objects such as chocolate bars, sausages, croissants or chocolate bananas imply the shape of a handle so as to be grasped with one hand and bitten off at the narrow side. To eat a fish finger differently to its geometrically indicated function would, for example, mean taking its narrow sides in both hands and biting along the middle of its long edge. A groove prompts the eater to break the object along that line, i.e., it elicits a certain behavior. To break off food that has breaking grooves any other way than along its edges would, in the sense of the product language, be a misinterpretation or show a disregard for the communicated user manual. The biscotti, known in English as the "Ladyfinger," is called "Löffelbiskuit" (spoon biscuit) in German because its shape resembles a teaspoon and so suggests a similar use.

Even the principle of "finger food" is often mediated by the nature of its design, though not as clearly as in the case of the breaking grooves. Whether a dish is intended to be finger food or not can usually be recognized via certain design features: if small items of four to five bites at most, made of a base substance like dough or similar, are held together so that they won't dirty or burn your fingers, it indicates that they should be eaten with the fingers and put in the mouth without cutlery.

In general, however, indicating functions are also an example of the fact that any separation into aesthetic, technical and symbolic function is purely theoretical and cannot be carried out so clearly in practice. Indicating functions operate via aesthetic characteristics (color, material, shape), communicates as a sign and conveys technical content; i.e., is both an aesthetic function (a specific form or condition) and is also a technical (fulfills a practical purpose – facilitating use) as well as communicative (conveys previously learned data) function. Strictly speaking, indicating functions are thus not a practical-technical function but a clear example that in the perception and use of objects, communication between object and human being always takes place simultaneously on all three levels: the aesthetic nature communicates (a previously learned) content which facilitates the (intended) use.

Summary

But back to the practical-technical functions of food: these include every measure taken to improve the use of food and drink – from processing it to eating it to waste disposal. What is deemed "better" in any specific case is a question of the ideology that determines the behavior. The fulfillment of practical functions influences the appearance of food as well as the way we relate to it, and offers a second, core motivation for food design in addition to the design of the sensory experience.

Symbolic function: Food as a ritual object

Design objects are always fulfilling symbolic functions in addition to aesthetic and practical-technical ones. By eating, we are not only consuming calories, but also connecting with a value system, because a "form in its material and visual presence always expresses (something to somebody). Signification can be regarded as a relation and interaction between the form and the person who perceives it.[89] There is no such thing as a meaningless item, and so there is no meaningless food. For us to put something in our mouth, it has to "nourish in a symbolic, social and emotional way as well as physically."[90]

In addition to the material intake of nutrients, an immaterial digestion of higher-level meanings takes place when we eat. The purpose of food goes far beyond the primary purpose of eating as the means of providing nutrients, because cuisine – that is, the food and drink typically available in a given environment – is "the sum of regional nutritional habits that depict social interaction and the common symbolic universe as much as the material environment."[91] The German philosopher Harald Lemke talks about gastro-theological symbolism and offers as an example how food is reduced to a purely symbolic function during holy communion.[92] A further example is the consumption of offal such as brains, heart or testicles, through which the bestowal of strength and wisdom or potency is promised to the eater.[93] Even aphrodisiacs or modern foods such as certain yogurt-based or energy drinks clearly fulfill recognizable, symbolic functions in which they not only satisfy hunger, but (are supposed to) also make you healthy, strong or beautiful.[94]

Shapes and other properties of products – whether they be food or other objects – are associated with meanings that can be understood or deciphered by a particular group of people based on a personal or socially-acquired body of experience. "Design creates a visual convention in the interaction between human participants both individually and collectively, thus enabling communication. Design is orientation."[95] The decision to use an object – to eat it in this particular case – depends not only on its usability (edibility) and its taste, but also on whether someone can understand and make use of the "signs" emanating from the object. People who are unfamiliar with Catholic tradition would not eat a nearly tasteless and calorie-free communion wafer. The German chemist and science journalist Jost Herbig writes: "Over the course of their socialization, each new generation acquired the collective knowledge of their ancestors encoded in religious systems. They used it in the course of their lives, tried it out, and passed it on perhaps slightly adjusted to their descendants. [...] The tried-and-tested individual patterns of behavior within the group, those of the group within larger organizations and in relation to nature, consolidated into cultural traditions as the centuries passed."[96] "While what is learned by chimpanzees represents personal knowledge, in humans it is shaped by the supra-personal knowledge of their culture."[97]

Ritual foods and other traditional food products demonstrate how people use the design of objects to convey meaning and make connections with an immaterial universe. "Design translates the functions of a commodity's pragmatic, semantic, affective nature by a congenial interpretation into a sign that the users can understand. The aim of the design is to make an object 'visible' and 'readable' so that communication becomes possible."[98]

Among the oldest surviving examples of food design are offerings of bread dough, the shape of which acts as a sign that conveys a higher meaning. During religious meals, "very ordinary and everyday actions are ritualized in such a way that, for example, a mundane meal is transformed into a sacred one. Offerings come from the same origins as religious meals. The point of sacrificial feasts and meals, [...], was to bring participants into the closest possible connection with divinity."[99] The particular appearance and condition of the offering helped to make this connection take place. It explains among other things the effort put into making bread in the shape of various animals such as fish, which was being baked from dough in Syria as early as ca. 1800 B.C. The Swiss art historian Andreas Morel mentions the "aesthetic optimization" of food.[100] Some of these symbolic food objects, such as braided bread – which probably developed as a substitute for the ancient offering of hair – still exist today, although their significance has largely been forgotten.[101]

Pretzels are another example of how culinary objects can carry meaning, act as signs and communicate. With its swirly, peculiar shape, the pretzel is a bakery product which is distinctive not for its taste or ingredients, but because of its special design. Its distinctive shape evolved from Roman ring loaves, which were used in early Christian times as sacramental pastries. German bread expert Max Währen has documented the use of pretzels during mass from the early Middle Ages and beyond, and has collected countless historical examples of different ring-loaf shapes right up to the eight that are in common use today.[102] Generally speaking, ring loaves may have originally been replicas of metal grave goods like bracelets (brazetella), which may explain their original ritual significance.[103] The pretzel in its present form has been in existence since at least the Middle Ages.[104]

To summarize, it is fair to say that people have been putting a great deal of effort into designing their food for thousands of years. We use our creativity and ingenuity to adapt nature's own products to our needs. The three key motivating factors in the design of food are to enhance sensory enjoyment when eating, to fulfill all kinds of technical-functional aspects and to transmit content and meaning.

1   Guixé, 2010, p. 113

2   See Stummerer, Hablesreiter, 2010, p. 13

3   Catterall, 1999, p. 23

4   Barlösius, 1999, p. 82

5   Sorgo, 2010, p. 69

6   See Jonas, 2007, p. 1364

7   Guixé, 2010, p. 112

8   See Wrangham, 2009

9   See Paczensky, Dünnebier, 1999, pp. 14–15

10   See Wrangham, 2009, p. 11

11   See Wrangham, 2009, p. 2

12   See Prahl, Setzwein, 1999, p. 34

13   Rigotti, 2003, p. 55

14   Paczensky, Dünnebier, 1999, p. 15

15   See Stummerer, Hablesreiter, 2010, pp. 14ff

16   Catterall, 1999, p. 23

17   See e.g., Gniech, 2002, p. 4

18   See Bauer Bauer-Wabnegg, 1997, p. 102

19   Papanek, 1984, p. 7

20   See Skone, 2010

21   From Böhme, 1995, p. 242

22   See Stummerer, Hablesreiter, 2010, p. 14

23   Schneider, 2009, p. 198

24   Schneider, 2009, p. 198

25   See Spence, 2017, p. 72

26   Korsmeyer, 2002, p. 40

27   See Korsmeyer, 2002, p. 41 and Grimm, 1984

28   See Plattig, 1995, pp. 11, 19, 21 and Vilgis, 2009, p. 14

29   See Vilgis, 2009, pp. 14, 22–23 and Plattig, 1995, pp. 36–38

30   See Muttenthaler, Limbeck-Lilienau, 2008, p. 108 and Plattig, 1995, pp. 36–44

31   See Spence, 2017, p. xx

32   See Plattig, 1995, pp. 11–12

33   See Spence, 2017, p. 21, Vilgis, 2008, pp. 16 and 24 and Plattig, 1995, pp. 12, 15, 32

34   See Plattig, 1995, pp. 72–73

35   See Kaufmann, 2005, p.16 and Korsmeyer, 2002, p. 103

36   Vilgis, 2008, p. 22

37   Korsmeyer, 2002, p. 6

38   See Plattig, 1995, pp. 72–73

39   See Eco, 1968

40   See Korsmeyer, 2002, p. 64

41   Wimmer, 2005, p. 41

42   See Stummerer, Hablesreiter, 2010, pp. 108 and 120 and Spence, 2017, p. 70

43   See Vilgis, 2008, p. 20

44   See Schneider, 2009, p. 198

45   See Dürrschmid, 2009, p. 21

46   See Dürrschmid, 2009, p. 4

47   See Langer, 1954, p. 72

48   See Bense, 1971, p. 36

49   See Langer, 1954, pp. 72–73

50   See Dürrschmid, 2009, p. 4

51   See Dürrschmid, 2009, p. 8

52   See Dürrschmid, 2009, pp. 4 and 7

53   See Barthes, 1961, p. 978

54   Barthes, 1957, Le bifteck et les frites

55   See Plattig, 1995, p.72–73 and Hahl, 2001, p. 8

56   See Dürrschmid, 2009, p. 9

57   See Davidson, 2006, p. 131

58   See Elschenbroich, 2010, p. 90, Schneider, 2009, p. 24

59   See Baudrillard, 1968

60   See Antonelli, 1999, pp. 54–63; Barilla, 2001, pp. 59ff

61   Stummerer, Hablesreiter, 2010, p. 124

62   Levine, 2009, p. 67

63   See Schneider, 2009, p. 198

64   See Paczensky, Dünnebier, 1999, pp. 437ff

65   See Grigorieva, 2015, pp. 678ff

66   See Stummerer, Hablesreiter, 2010, p. 14

67   Steffen, 1995, p. 10

68   Erlhoff, Marshall, 2008, keyword function

69   Blochel-Dittrich, 2009, p. 77

70   See Lemke, 2007, p. 87

71   Blochel-Dittrich, 2009, p. 77

72   See Lemke, 2007, p. 87

73   See Thallemer, 2011, p. 216

74   See Erlhoff, Marshall, 2008, keyword function

75   See Gudrun Scholz in Steffen, 1995, p. 24

76   Brandes, Stich, Wender, 2009, p. 55

77   See Schneider, 2009, p. 39

78   See Erlhoff, Marshall, 2008, keyword function

79   See Papanek, 1984, p. 6

80   See Schneider, 2009, p. 39

81   See Schneider, 2009, p. 203

82   See Brandes, Stich, Wender, 2009, p. 56

83   See Langer, 1954, pp. 23–24

84   See Steffen, 2000, p. 62

85   See Steffen, 2000, pp. 62ff and Brandes, Stich, Wender, 2009, p. 56

86   Steffen, 2000, p. 63

87   Steffen, 2000, p. 63

88   See Lorenzer, 1981, p. 155

89   Vihma, 2007, pp. 225 and 227

90   Sorgo, 2010, p. 70

91   Sorgo, 2010, p. 70

92   See Lemke, 2007, pp. 84–85

93   See Hirschfelder, 2005, p. 34

94   See Sorgo 2010 (2), p. 50

95   Meier, 2003, p. 12

96   Herbig, 1988, p. 71

97   Herbig, 1988, p. 89

98   Schneider, 2009, p. 197

99   Barlösius, 1999, p. 193

100   See Morel, 2001, p. 12

101   See Korsmeyer, 2002, p. 126, Hansen, 1968, p. 31 and Döbler, 2002, p. 89

102   See Währen, 2000, pp. 623ff and Blochel-Dittrich, 2009, p. 75

103   See Hansen, 1968, p. 31

104   See Währen, 2000, p. 579

Food products (and their design) as signs: Higher meanings of food products

"Design must be meaningful."[1]

"The enrichment of food with added meaning – like food itself – is an anthropological constant, though the food in question and its connotations may vary a great deal from culture to culture."[2]

Introduction

Food appears in a wide variety of shapes, colors, textures and tastes. As in other areas of everyday life – be it clothing, housing or fine dining – our ancestors have conceived countless edible items (dishes, drinks, recipes, etc.) to fulfill the basic human need for "food."[3] The multitude of items available bears no rational connection to their actual purpose: we could also get by with far fewer and more simply designed objects in our daily lives. So what motivates people to design food in so many different ways? "How come we make things and surround ourselves with such abundance? Why do we spend so much time and effort on them and worry so much when the loss – or even a disruption in the order – of our material environment is threatened [...]?"[4]

The effort people put into the design of food is disproportionate to its physical use as a provider of sustenance and cannot be explained by it. Is there a rational reason why bread dough or pasta is formed into so many different shapes, when it makes no difference – or hardly any difference – to its nutritional value and taste but is significantly harder to produce?

Eating is an everyday activity, but certainly not a meaningless one. Countless decisions are necessarily made before every meal. The choice of basic ingredients, how they are prepared and eaten as well as the condition of the food are cultural (not natural) processes that, albeit perhaps subconsciously, have been brought about by humans (and not by nature). Food that has been specifically prepared and shaped has been communicating symbolic content and signaling affiliation to interest groups and communities for millennia. In ancient Egypt, bread was shaped into pyramids or fish, transforming it into offerings.[5] To this day, food design is far more cultural than practical.

In addition to their role as sustenance, edible items play a very important symbolic role within a group. "In choosing their belongings [by eating them in the case of food] or what things they do not own [do not eat], people are constantly giving signs for others to decipher. At a cultural level, they are committed to certain traditions and rituals [e.g., preparation methods, cooking recipes, traditional dishes, table manners]. At a social level, it is about status and belonging to a group, and on an individual level about the sentimental attachment to objects."[6]

Every item – whether edible or not – always has symbolic value in addition to its use value. When we eat, not only do we consume the calorific value of the eaten object, but we also use it as an emotional, social and existence-legitimizing opportunity for expression.[7] In many cases, the design of food does not serve to supply the body with calories, but to give signs. From shrimp cocktail to doner kebab; from ciabatta to instant soup: What we consume is not necessarily just a question of taste, but also of symbolism.

Even if the design of food is motivated to some extent by enjoyment and functional considerations, the deciding factor in whether a type of food is ultimately successful is its symbolism. By "successful" we don't mean economic success in this context; but rather how often, over what period of time and by how many people a food or a dish is consumed in the course of its history. And a type of food only becomes successful when the food in question suits the incumbent worldview, set of values and attitude to life, because even if something tastes really good and works really well, it will only be eaten if it communicates the "right" things. According to Roland Barthes, needs are transformed into values in the process of eating.

For him, food is not only a representation of certain motives, but also of situations; in short, of a lifestyle.[8]

Food products and their design not only have a social impact – be it communal or stratifying[9] – but also a meaningful effect.[10] Cultural objects (food, in this case) are understood to be the essence of living socially: "as remnants of a past world that we still see before us as blueprints for our own lives."[11] Just like other cultural objects, food that is prepared and presented in a certain way allows the "sensory experience of a realized blueprint of life" and assuages "the yearning for a world that satisfies the senses."[12] One task that food symbolism fulfils is to generate a system that makes decisions easier and specifies patterns of behavior. The design signifies adherence to certain procedural criteria in the culinary rulebook which demonstrate the group's usual dietary practices and help the individual decide what, when and how he or she should eat, or even makes the decision entirely on their behalf.

However, meanings within food are not necessarily related to nutrition; they can convey all kinds of content and values from all walks of life. The design, from the selection of ingredients to the method of preparation to how it is shaped, elicits ideas which produce associations of meaning to topics that may be outside the sphere of nutrition.[13]

(Attempt at a) theory of object language

People shape and realize everything they encounter, including their food. Designs – whether of food products or other objects – communicate content that can be understood or decoded by a given group of people based on culturally acquired knowledge. The design of food forms part of a pool of social knowledge, which is partly transmitted to the subjective knowledge pool of the individual members, where it in turn forms part of his or her general pool of knowledge. Food, or its design, can function as a sign and transmit collective, tacit knowledge in this way. Since a large proportion of the subjective pool of knowledge does not come from first-hand experience but represents knowledge conveyed by other persons,[14] the question arises of whether and how objects – including food – can participate in such processes of knowledge transfer.

Why food and dishes are designed the way they are (and not differently) can be explained, among other things, by the meanings attributed to certain modes of design. In order to examine the symbolic nature of objects, i.e., the style and sense of how things – in this case food products – are related to ideas, we would like to draw on the following two concepts: design semantics based on the theory of signs (semiotics) and American philosopher Susanne Langer's Theory of Symbolism.

"Zeichen und Design" (Sign and design)

"Zeichen und Design" – is the title of a 1971 book by German philosopher Max Bense. The semiotic concept of signs, based on the theories of American philosopher Charles Sanders Peirce, was seized on by design theory in the 1950s and carried forward by Max Bense among others, and later by Finnish theorist Susann Vihma in design research.[15]

In design semantics, the theory of signs is used as a method of analyzing the semantic dimension of design objects (by means of interpretation). Susann Vihma writes: "[…] it is clear, that design always comprises a semantic dimension which is not measurable in the same way as the other three [being construction and technology, use and material], because semantic analysis is about interpretation and requires other means for its study."[16] consequently, for Susann Vihma symbols are "a useful theoretical tool for analysis."[17] In the German-speaking world, Max Bense was the pioneering figure in introducing the concept of signs to design theory. Bense (1910–1990) was an accomplished physicist, chemist, mathematician and philosopher who worked in both scientific and humanities disciplines; on the theory of science, logic, aesthetics and semiotics among others. He taught semiotics at the Ulm School of Design in the 1950s, resulting in his work being recognized in German (and later also international) design. Max Bense's work has been incorporated into design theory, where his concept of signs remains valid to this day. German art scholar Cordula Meier, for example, refers to Max Bense when she calls for teaching linguistic skills within the context of university design education: "Since Max Bense, and earlier, we have understood the connection between seeing, conceptualizing and speaking."[18] And Susann Vihma's definition of the four dimensions of design (syntax, semantics, pragmatics and material), which she established as the basis for the development of a semiotic view of design, was inspired by her own account by reading Max Bense's "Sign and Design" (1971).[19]

In the wake of Charles S. Peirce, Bense sees signs in terms of a triadic ratio, i.e., as a relationship between a means M, an object reference O and an interpreter I. For Bense, a sign Z is a means M denoting an object O which means something to an interpretant I.[20] Susann Vihma summarizes the process of forming signs (also based on Peirce's theory) as follows: "The semiotic process of producing signs can be explained in a simplified way as an interpretation of something that relates to something else."[21] Signs are therefore the relationship between M, O, and I, where M is that which represents, O is the symbolic content and I the process of interpretation (not the interpretive individual). In other words, "In semiotics, a sign represents something in some capacity, when it is interpreted. It follows that a sign consists of relations between three components: that which represents (Representamen) something (the reference, content), and the interpretative act."[22] However, this process only works if the interpreter has the appropriate repertoire of signs, because signs always only work in relation to other signs, or are based on a repertoire of signs, or on an interrelationship between signs[23] (which could also be called culture). According to Vihma, it is important in the analysis of design objects not to confuse the sign with the material object: "A sign is not a thing, but a theory about relations."[24] In the act of interpretation, a person generates various types of reference relationships. It is not the product itself (the designed object) that refers to some kind of meaningful content, but a corresponding interpretation that establishes a relationship to some meaningful content. The object is only the medium that elicits interpretations by means of its shape, color and materiality: "A material product can carry meanings when interpreted."[25]

Sign and symbol (representation)

The second theory that we want to put forward here, which has also contributed significantly to (German) design semantics, is US philosopher Susanne Langer's theory of symbolism. In design, Langer's theory is most renowned for establishing the concept of indicating functions, but in addition to this the Offenbach approach to product language is also based on Langer's theory among others.[26]

Langer basically distinguishes between signs that indicate things and signs that represent things. While animals are able to learn simple indicators, the formation of symbols – that is, signs that refer to things that are not present – is a typically human ability.[27] The perception of a thing or a situation in terms of a symbol means using it to evoke the mere idea of it (or something associated with it) without it actually being physically there. This is the only way thinking or communicating about absent things, events in the past or in the future, and abstract concepts is even possible. While animals only understand sounds, gestures, and objects as indication of actual things or immediate events, and actions in the here and now, people can also interpret things symbolically. In humans, things and sensory stimuli generally always have a twofold effect: firstly as indicators that control behavior (like with animals), and simultaneously as symbols that do not require an immediate response. This symbolic understanding, this ability to consciously evoke the idea of an absent thing or a faraway event is what makes it even possible to think or talk about something that isn't physically present. The dual processing of the same sensory data as an indicator on one hand and a symbol on the other is the prerequisite for comprehension, thinking and intelligence. Paradoxically, the conclusions drawn as a result of the dual interpretation of what is being perceived need not necessarily complement one another in a coherent image: the different levels of meaning can also contradict each other, reinforce each other or cancel each other out.[28]

Language and design

"Not only are language and design similar in structure, but they are closely intertwined with each other. Design is based on language."[29]

Like the elements of verbal language, material things also transmit messages via the way they are designed or regarded, and are understood as signs by the observer who perceives and interprets these things. Design semantics and product language, which address the symbolic quality of objects, have been a theme in design research since the 1980s.[30] The term "product language," which came from business management, was appropriated for design theory in 1973 by German art educator Gert Selle and subsequently developed mainly by Jochen Gros and Dagmar Steffen.[31] The concept of product language stems from the critique of modernity and the debate on functionalism, which with its motto "form follows function" had petered out by itself into a formalism after a few decades. As a consequence, the idea of incorporating the representational alongside the practical-technical functions emerged; symbolic and aesthetic functions became important parameters in design activity.[32] The discourse about style and the future focus of design was also influenced and inspired by developments in other areas (including literature, semiotics and postmodernism). In English-speaking countries, the term "product semantics" has been in use since the 1980s, having been coined in 1984 by Klaus Krippendorff and Reinhart Butter.[33] Klaus Krippendorff sees product semantics as a conceptual tool for designers – a kind of vocabulary – for constructively engaging in the manufacture of meaning. Product semantics is therefore "a systematic inquiry into how people attribute meanings to artifacts and interact with them accordingly and a vocabulary and methodology for designing artifacts in view of the meanings they could acquire for their users and the communities of their stakeholders."[34] The ultimate ideological question of which principles should guide the design of objects led to a search to establish a theoretical foundation for the symbolic function of objects, resulting in the theory of product language or design semantics.

The core question of design semantics is "how the artifact expresses, represents, refers to and embodies the symbolic content."[35] For German product designer and design theorist Jochen Gros, professor of design theory at the University of Art and Design in Offenbach am Main (1974–2004) who was significantly involved in developing the theory of product language (the Offenbach approach), product language is a process that plays out between the object and the percipient; that is, one which does not progress exclusively from one to the other, but is an interplay between the two. Hence, meaning is not a property that is inherent in an object, but rather arises through the relationship between people and objects.[36] This is a point of view which is also argued by Finnish theoretician Susann Vihma: What artifacts refer to – their meaning – is, according to Vihma, not "somewhere outside the product or the perceiver, but in the relationship between them."[37] The concept of "embodiment" suggests a connection between mediation and design; that is, the indivisible unity of form and meaning. If an object were merely a representation of ideas, it would imply an arbitrariness or an independence from the physical properties of the medium and the mediated content.

The term embodiment, however, clarifies the fact that an object's attributes are the main instrument of mediation; content cannot be transported independently of the object and its design. "Reference relations – simply called signs in semiotics – do not function as a substitute for reality, but are an innate part of the actual thing itself, are the sensations and perceptions that it evokes."[38]

In bringing forward her philosophical concept into design theory, Susanne Langer's concept of "representation" is broadened into the idea of "embodying": This is because in a purely linguistic sense, an object expresses something, conveys or refers to its meaning; it symbolizes (represents) it. In terms of design, however, it also embodies it. The conceptual translation from Langer's "representation" to Vihma's "embodiment" arises from the perspective of the relationship between objects and people: while philosophy operates from a human perspective and sees objects as a means of representing human thought, design theory puts objects at the center of attention. By embodying something, they – not just people – take an active role in the communication of product language.

Object language

Objects have symbolic qualities comparable to those of spoken language, and are in no way inferior in their expressiveness, significance, and cultural complexity.[39] "Design can easily be treated as a sort of symbolic system likened to verbal narrative and storytelling."[40] But to what extent can object language really be compared to conventional language?

Differences between language and object language; object language is not arbitrary and non-linear

Language in the classical sense has a vocabulary and a syntax. It is discursive and consists of fixed units of meaning (words). According to the rules of syntax, the elements of vocabulary – words – can be combined into larger units such as sentences, whole texts, etc.; i.e., into new symbols with a given meaning. The same content can be expressed in a variety of ways, enabling the meaning of the symbols to be specified by synonyms or combinations of other words in the form of a dictionary. The fixed meanings of the individual words allow them to be defined and make them decipherable. Translations into other languages are therefore possible.[41]

Unlike traditional language, picture and object language are not discursive. While language breaks down and times all content to deliver it one step at a time in a strictly orderly sequence, object language sends out an abundance of data simultaneously. This has the advantage of being able to be grasped much more quickly and directly, and also generates a different quality of understanding on the emotional level. It is therefore especially apt for conveying ideas that cannot be expressed through language. On the other hand, a three-dimensional design language cannot be translated into discursive language without there being shifts of meaning – which may sometimes be minor and sometimes even result in a total loss of meaning – and can therefore only be partially accessible to discursive thought.[42] Content that cannot be broken down into sequential units cannot be transmitted using conventional language. In a very real sense, then, it cannot be "put into words."

Individual elements

Design language also has a vocabulary, because the integral design of an object consists of many smaller, meaningful units such as color, surface, material, etc. Object language has far more elements to it than conventional language, however. Its meaning is not clear and lucid like that of words and sentences, but vague and imprecise, and offers tremendous scope for interpretation. It is not possible to draw reliable conclusions about the meaning of a given facet based on the meaning of the selfsame facet in another context, and neither does the relationship between the content and the symbol denoting it have to be mutual. If, for example, the color "yellow" stands for "freshness," "health" or "attention" in a given context, it doesn't necessarily follow that it can be used in a different context to convey the word "freshness" (or health, attention, etc.). There can therefore be no dictionary of picture or design language, because the symbolism of each facet varies depending on the context.[43]

According to Langer, visual forms such as lines, colors and proportions can occur in the most varied of combinations; i.e., they can be abstracted and combined. They are just as good as words for articulating and making complex combinations.[44] In our culture, the smallest unit of language is a letter. It is meaningless in itself (in the explicit sense it just indicates itself; it can certainly have implicit meaning, for example as a logo). Without context, it cannot convey meaning. With object language, on the other hand, the smallest unit of meaning cannot even be clearly identified as it is dependent on context, so it cannot be fixed. Even the smallest distinguishing marks such as e.g., a scratch or kink can be meaningful. Without context, technical, material, visual or any other sensory facets can neither exist nor be detected (there is no color without form, etc.). The individual units that carry meaning can therefore be neither isolated nor universally quantified. It would be impossible to single out a system of basic units of information that could be compiled like a dictionary from the multitude of communication processes that occur simultaneously at all five sensory levels. Moreover, with the vast majority of objects the implicit – i.e., subconsciously transmitted – meaning far outweighs the explicit, i.e. expressed meaning (e.g., crescent shape for moon). This means that what makes sense is not only dependent on context, but is also subject to greater subjective variability (the same signal has a different meaning to different perceivers). Implicit meaning is generally harder to conventionalize than explicit because it is non-conceptual[45] and cannot therefore be comprehensively and directly communicated verbally. Basically, knowledge does not have to be articulated (or otherwise objectified) verbally. Experiential knowledge, for example, is largely pre-linguistic,[46] but this does not mean that it isn't a form of knowledge. The same is generally true of the experiences we have when tasting and eating and the knowledge we have gathered in the process. It is merely harder to pin down this knowledge because extra-linguistic knowledge can only be indirectly talked about. Two people will most likely never taste the same food in the same way;[47] only they do not know it because they cannot use language to communicate it. The perception of taste is for the most part a form of tacit knowledge, which in contrast to explicit knowledge is difficult to communicate verbally since it cannot be explicitly expressed (for example, verbalized) – or at least, only to a limited extent.[48] For many of our sensory perceptions, moreover, we have a barely developed spoken vocabulary (i.e., that can be used for translating into explicit knowledge). This means there is simply a lack of appropriate words that can be extensively used to express e.g., smell and taste impressions in detail, whereas by comparison there is a far more diverse vocabulary for describing, say, visual perceptions.

Ambiguity – relativity

Wordless symbols are untranslatable and non-discursive. Because of the ambiguity of simultaneously transmitted sensory signals, any translation into conventional language or into visuals or otherwise-transmitted synonyms does not work, or only works with a significant loss of meaning. The meaning ascribed to the elements is flexible and varies according to context, which makes clearly defining the elements impossible.[49] Though design vocabulary consists of different elements, these are only loosely and not immutably linked to meanings, and this link can change depending on the context. According to Bense, signs are by their very nature always thetical (i.e., made, formulated; a thesis or an assertion), selective and relative, i.e., weakly determined or extremely indefinite.[50] Moreover, the elements of object language cannot be "transcribed," i.e., expressed or translated using other signs.[51] How interrelation/connectivity works between the carrier of signs and their content is ambiguous; in addition, the number of possible combinations is many times higher than with written or spoken language.

Ambiguous and non-specific wordless symbols, which could perhaps be seen as a disadvantage from a purely rational perspective, give in contrast to conventional language the advantage of being able to transmit certain content more easily. It is precisely object language's ambiguity that makes it apt for expressing, cultural things because "the excessive semantic density and ambiguous integrability of symbols make it possible to at least agree on the ambiguous due to competing interests."[52] Hence, the communication of cultural content is better suited to a language that has a strong symbolic character like object language as opposed to, say, a dry, scientific text – not least because of the wide scope of interpretation options.

"Thinking" in/with objects

The ambiguity of units of meaning as well as the simultaneous transmission of a wealth of signals, as happens in the case of object language, does not mean that design language doesn't convey content or that its content makes less sense or is less "intelligent" than linguistic content. Quite the contrary: The conclusion that design language is not rational, intelligent or cognitive because it is not translatable into discursive thinking is fundamentally wrong, according to Langer. Knowledge gained through the senses, intuition or inspiration is also rational;[53] merely subject to a different pattern of thought and comprehension than discursive thinking. Other sophisticated systems of thought also operate independently of conventional language, such as those of mathematics and physics; areas of knowledge that have developed their own system of symbols to represent their interpretation of reality. The symbols of sensory comprehension are not primitive precursors on the road to a higher way of understanding the world based on physical laws – the supposition of which Langer calls "a fatal error in epistemology"[54] – but are a particular mode of understanding; the very representation of reality through the abstractions of sensory perception. This reality differs from the physical interpretation of reality, but is no less real or relevant. Sensory perceptions – i.e., the abstractions performed by our eyes, our ears, or another sensory organ – are the most basic instruments of our intelligence. They certainly don't form part of discursive thought, but are a part of thought as a whole; they are the fundamental, "real" symbolic essence of thought:[55] "Typified experiences are doubtless something like elementary forms of knowledge."[56] Sensory comprehension takes place on the rational level of thought, as does physical-mathematical or any other method of understanding. Sensory abstractions are indeed the very symbolic transformations that provide the raw material for all kinds of mental activities. They are the first medium of "understanding" that allows us to convey things and events and be able to recognize and grasp them: "Rationality is the essence of mind, and symbolic transformation its elemental process."[57] Sensory understanding, intuition or artistic truth represent another mode of thinking. Because they work with symbolizations, they are the result of a cognitive, i.e., rational process and do not fall into the realm of feelings or emotion. Even the incredible feat of comprehending the flood of impressions that bombard our sensory organs and transforming them into specific ideas and events is a process of abstraction that cannot be accomplished through language-based thinking. A space, for example, cannot be readily understood even by a comprehensive, discursive knowledge of its geometry.[58] It requires "sensory" thinking, which is also nature's mode of thinking; that of the objective world itself and of design as well. The perception of taste is also a rational process. If something tastes "sour," for example, it is not a sensory perception or a feeling, but the recognition of a symbolic form, namely the symbolic form "sour." For the eater, food never lacks meaning. All sensory stimuli associated with consuming a food product – be it taste, smell, appearance, texture, chewing sound, temperature or tenderness – are assembled into a cognitive-emotional association of meaning in the brain,[59] i.e., abstracted into symbolic forms.

The building blocks of meaning need not necessarily be spoken or written language, but can also consist of material objects: Any random material can arbitrarily be endowed with meaning.[60] For Barthes, the "materials" of mythical expression are language, photography, painting, posters, ritual, object, etc. There are other systems as well as spoken and written language existing within a group able to convey content and transmit knowledge. One of these is design, product or "object language."[61] German sociologist Hubert Knoblauch talks about "material objects," which can serve as objectifications in the same way as phonetic signs or images.[62]

Roland Barthes

One of the first thinkers to systematically analyze food through its symbolism was the French literary theorist Roland Barthes (1915–1980). In "Mythologies" (1957), Barthes examines everyday objects and their meanings with a chapter explicitly dedicated to food; namely steak and fries.[63] In 1961, Roland Barthes even published an essay entitled "Pour une psycho-sociologie de l'alimentation contemporaine" (Toward a Psychosociology of Contemporary Food Consumption), which deals exclusively with the subject of food. Barthes was interested in all kinds of language systems and in how sense and meaning arise in different language systems. His work addresses everyday (including industrial) products among others, and how they convey meaning.[64] Using structuralist, deconstructivist and psychoanalytic techniques, he analyzed daily phenomena including writing, movies, fashion, advertising, love – and also food. Barthes inspired design theory – especially design semiotics and product semantics – with his approach of moving everyday objects into the focus of scientific observation and perceiving and interpreting them as carriers of meaning (i.e., signs). Barthes and his systematic consideration and analysis of everyday objects are often used in design literature: including e.g., by Finnish theoretician Susann Vihma in connection with the conceptual explanation of "product semantics" and the fundamental questions that pertain to it,[65] or by German design theorist Dagmar Steffen in connection with objects as signs.[66]

Unity of form and content – arbitrariness

The way objects act as units of a non-verbal "object language" – as Barthes calls it – differs in some respects from the way verbal language works. Verbal language basically works arbitrarily: i.e., the relationship between the official carrier of a symbol and its designated meaning is arbitrary. The idea of language being arbitrary goes back to Swiss linguist Ferdinand de Saussure. He claimed that in spoken and written language, the relationship between a sound- or typeface is man-made and not natural (though there are some exceptions; so-called "relative motivation," e.g., onomatopoeic words). The association of a particular articulation of sounds to a concept is based on convention (habit, tradition). In linguistics, the theory of conventionalism is in opposition to that of naturalism, which argues for a natural/given connection between sound image and designated thing.

As opposed to spoken language, image and object language is not arbitrary: although visual (haptic, olfactory, etc.) signs are continuously evolving and are formed in the day-to-day practice of traditions and conventions, there is however a fundamental link between material form and transmitted meaning. A form always means something to someone,[67] if only because it cannot offer a purely sensory experience that precedes cognition in the brain and exists independently of it. All sensory impressions are only converted into conscious perceptions in the brain, and this process always follows within the framework of a complex system of experience, expectation, memory, emotion and knowledge.[68] The fact that a form always implies something in object language is another key difference to verbal language.

A random assortment of letters, sounds or words from conventional language cannot yield words or coherent sentences and thus make no sense, i.e., it is meaningless: By "meaningless" we mean in the sense of explicit language (syntax). Of course, it may have a formal-aesthetic meaning, e.g., as a logo or a graphic; as onomatopoeia or as vocals (for example yodeling). By contrast, the combination of material and physical design elements always conveys something. If the form changes in a given associative link between a particular shape (e.g., a crescent-shaped pastry) and the content it conveys ("croissant") – for example to a straight pastry – then this changes the content, but the form doesn't become meaningless; it just conveys something else.

In the case of object language, the medium and the object reference – or the information and the sign carrier – are inseparable, but determine each other. Langer notes that artistic symbols (as opposed to linguistic ones) cannot be translated because their meaning is tied to their specific form. Verbal language also tends to lose its arbitrariness when used artistically, as in poetry. In general, the idea of arbitrariness refers to the explicit content of speech and not to implicit mediators of meaning such as intonation, rhythm, etc., because spoken or written language always has an aesthetic appearance as well, and is always communicating implicit (non-linguistic) meaning simultaneously. In object language on the other hand, any sense or content is embedded in the object itself, i.e., implicitly, and cannot be made explicit by any kind of interpretation.[69] Meaning (object reference) and design (medium) form an inseparable whole; if one of the two elements are changed, the other changes as well. There is no content without form; conversely, unlike with language, there is no form without content.

In aesthetics, the question of content is also always a question of form.[70] The process of forming and recognizing signs (coding and decoding), i.e., the link between medium, object reference and interpretant[71] is always linked to the attributes – or the design – of the edible objects in question. Put simply: if you straighten out a croissant, it becomes a rod and no longer a croissant. And since the curved shape of the croissant is more than just a distinguishing feature (namely, a reference to the crescent moon) and "croissant" is more than just a name to distinguish it from other types of bakery product – i.e., is not only based on convention – a change in physical shape also results in a loss of meaning. The style, i.e., the aesthetic form, is part of the statement; moreover, it is the medium itself through which content, meaning and message is transported in the first place. If design superficially determines the aesthetics of an object, this process creates the true basis for the transmission of meanings. The meanings cannot be separated from the aesthetics, but they are conveyed by them. Aesthetics are the basic characteristics, the sensorially perceivable state of an object, which determine its function or allow and/or demand certain types of action, at the same time acting as a medium for the object's symbolism and transmitting meaning. The aesthetics – as well as the functionality – always convey meaning and are never meaningless.

Whether the meanings themselves are created or merely communicated during this process is a question of how you look at it: does meaning emerge as people perceive objects, or when people project independently existing meanings onto objects? Max Bense describes semiosis (making signs) as a generative process in which the medium (the material carrier of signs) produces the object reference (the object that is represented; the designated object) and it is only the object reference that evokes the interpretation or meaning.[72]

The difference between the croissant as a lunar and fertility symbol and steak with fries as a sign of Frenchness, as Roland Barthes describes it,[73] lies in the fact that the crooked shape of croissants (also) has an explicit meaning – namely as a reference to the moon; steak with French fries on the other hand has become a symbol of a certain way of life thanks to its common use: that is, as a convention over an extended period of time in France in the 1950s. These different levels of meaning always work together and, depending on the specific application example, express themselves with varying potency, and may even contradict each other. The croissant, for example, is on the one hand a depictive, iconic sign that denotes the moon; on the other hand, it is a symbolic sign (in reference to absent things and concepts, a context based on convention), for the meanings associated with the moon: e.g., fertility, moon goddess, divine power, etc., and the many more meanings its design conveys (including portion size, small white flour pastries, ergonomics, social use, etc.). The various meanings that the different levels of form communicate overlap each other in an image that is not always consistent (fixed / held together in the collective sink of the term "croissant"), which then filters down into current cultural use. The perceived meanings are the result of associations that are learned, i.e., from an interplay of forms and the content associated with them, from which the type of association can be more or less strongly conventionalized. However, they can never achieve the level of conventionalization of normal language, in which the forms are completely arbitrary (with a few exceptions) compared to content, i.e., they are interchangeable. The connection between the actual form and its meaning can never be completely independent of the design, since object language is not arbitrary. The meaning of steak and fries is also composed of an (endless) number of "partial symbols":

e.g., myths about meat, the symbolism of blood, the seared surface, the juicy core, the specific aroma, the juice-induced chewing sound, etc. Object language is always an interplay of iconic, indexical and symbolic meaning. This is true for both the entire object as well as the individual components of the object that carry meaning.

Language consists of symbols which are arrived by convention. If "real" symbols are only those which are based on convention (according to Peirce), then there are no objects that are purely symbols because content and form cannot be separated. While with verbal language, words and their meaning can be redefined – that is exchanged – this is not possible for objects because the content changes as the form changes. On the other hand, according to Langer perception means filtering out symbolic forms (namely which ones those are and what they look like) that are exclusively a product of convention. This means perception is symbolic and is solely a product of convention. Langer's basis for defining a symbol differs from that of the theory of symbols' founder, Charles Peirce: for Peirce the prerequisite for a symbol is that its meaning is merely a result of convention (such symbols cannot exist as material reality); for Langer a symbol is a reference to things, events, concepts etc. that are not present.

The number of characters object language has is infinite, not limited and fixed like the 26 letters of the alphabet or the words in a dictionary. This infinite number of possible characters and their ambiguity mean that even small changes in design lead to new content and meanings. A tiny change in the hue of sausage – e.g., just a hint of green – can cause it to appear off and no longer appealing. As well as the mandatory combination of shape, color and material, this infinite variety on the one hand and the ambiguity of forms on the other mean that the content and the means of expression (the object and its material manifestation) cannot be separated like in conventional language. This means: Object language is not arbitrary.

How the sensory experience of what is eaten relates to spiritual meaning can be demonstrated by the example of the communion wafer: The communion wafer is primarily a (purely) symbolic meal: it establishes a connection to ideas that are not present: Bread, Christ, sacrifice, etc. Through the consumption of a certain food – in this case, the communion wafer – an emotional link perceivable by the senses is made to a higher, abstract world of thought. The simple and practical design of the communion wafer, which is devoid of embellishment, does not at first glance reflect the general meaning of the communion wafer – i.e., the ritual consummation of God – and appears to be arbitrary in nature. On the other hand the lack of substance and the simple design, which can be interpreted as a distancing from earthly-material existence, correspond to the transcendent nature of consuming food for a symbolic and abstract purpose. The design of the communion wafer thus indeed mirrors its function in the sensory experience as a Catholic ritualistic food: "Its ephemeral physical form, its very subtle taste, the delicate material which does not need to be chewed but simply dissolves in the mouth"[74] and the virtually nonexistent nutritional value represent the sublimated body of Christ and the abstract sharing of food during the Holy Communion.[75]

Food as a sign

Objects have symbolic value. Insofar as every object is perceived and understood, rationally processed and associated with a purpose, it always "means" something.[76] According to Langer, "the assignment of elaborately patterned symbols to certain analogues in experience" is "the basis of all interpretation and thought."[77] As perception occurs, sensory data is transformed into concepts ("all thinking is conceptual, and conception begins with the comprehension of 'Gestalt'."[78]), understood through filters of previously learned and known "forms" ("Gestalten"), which in turn allows us to perceive at all. In the course of this process of identification, the forms perceived are usually categorized and labeled based on their type.[79]

Form ("Gestalt") always implies a meaning (otherwise we would not be able to perceive it as "something," but rather an undefined mishmash of sensory data). In any case, objects and also food thus have a meaning. In his essay "Pour une psycho-sociologie de l'alimentation contemporaine" (Toward a Psychosociology of Contemporary Food Consumption) Barthes basically asks: "What is food? Not merely a plethora of products governed by statistical and dietary studies; but also a communication system, a repository of images, use, response and behavioral guidelines."[80] Food becomes a symbol shared between the members of a certain group. "As soon as a need is governed by production and consumption guidelines – in other words, as soon as it becomes an institution – the function of the symbol can no longer be separated from its purpose; this applies to clothing a much as it does to food. From a (completely abstract) anthropological standpoint food is undoubtedly the primary need."[81]

Food practices involving everything from procuring up to consuming food are represented by a specific set of rules recognized and practiced by a certain group.[82] The actual implementation and legitimation of these rules occurs with the help of (culturally acquired) tastes ("tastes good") and other meanings ("healthy," "traditional," "ritual," etc.), that are attributed to edible items. For Barthes, systematizing the symbolism of alimentary items makes food a true means of communication within a group: "Substances, techniques, practices in turn produce a system of differences that generate meaning, at which point alimentary communication is established. What proves that we are dealing with communication is not the more-or-less alienated awareness that its users have of it, but the readiness with which nutritional factors form a structure analogous to other communication systems."[83] By their nature or design (which is perceived as a visual, haptic, acoustic, olfactory and/or gustatory sensory impression), food products transmit content and meaning, and pass on knowledge: "The reality is (need or pleasure), [...] that food is the carrier of a communication system: It is not the only object that people continue to experience as merely a function, while at the same time making it a sign."[84] This knowledge is for the most part implicit; i.e., it is acquired and passed on without language and can only be transformed into explicit knowledge to a limited extent,[85] whereas all explicit knowledge contains a large amount of tacit knowledge.[86] The accumulation of such a repository of knowledge (in this specific case the way food is designed) takes place selectively, according to Berger and Luckmann. It is passed on from generation to generation and is available to individuals who are members of the group or culture in question. Such individuals are equipped with a normal share of knowledge, and know that others know the same thing; at least to some extent. Interaction in the everyday world is determined by the fact that people share in the same repository of knowledge. This also makes it possible to classify an individual within the group, which cannot be done with someone who does not share in the repository of knowledge.[87]

The symbolic content of food

What can food tell us about the structure of language, and how can its meanings be described? Why people are in favor of or against eating certain dishes and drinks – that is, which ideas people associate with them – firstly depends on the (apparently) simplest basis for making these decisions: perceiving an object through the senses. Before we decide in favor of or against something, we must first perceive it. "An object is not a datum, but a form construed by the sensitive and intelligent organ, a form which is at once an experienced individual thing and a symbol for the concept of it, for this sort of thing."[88]

Concept and convention

A set of object properties that make a particular food or dish recognizable as such is what identifies the object itself, or the notion we have of it. Product language tells of essential features which indicate the type of product via a specific number and selection of indicators.[89] Edible objects are not only material objects but also concepts; i.e., a more-or-less clearly defined set of ideas. All items that can be included under a concept, symbolize this concept. Whether we're talking about scrambled eggs, hamburgers or frozen pizzas: these items not only exist physically over the course of their lifespan, but also as idealized objects in the imagination of the people who are familiar with the concept. A dish or drink has to – within certain parameters – be made in a certain way so that it is recognized as a cake, pretzel, soup or schnitzel. If the properties of the object deviate too much from this conception, it will not be recognized as such: e.g., a doughnut without hole. Of course, this principle not only works for the designation of foodstuffs, but also for material objects of all kinds: For example, a door must have certain attributes in order to be regarded as a door, and naturally there are always gray areas among both edible and non-edible objects. Furthermore, the entire system operates on the basis of use and convention within a particular social framework – and is constantly shifting. The food itself then becomes the meaning that the sign conveys: If you want to make a pretzel, certain design criteria must be met so that the product is recognized at the end as a pretzel and conveyed with the meanings associated with the concept "pretzel," such as a certain common use, a link to extra-culinary systems, etc.

Since food objects change through use on the one hand and naturally decay on the other, they tend to change over time – this also applies to their symbolic meaning. Food products go through different stages of their existence: for example from raw ingredients, to dough, to the product, to crumbs, to stomach contents, and finally the separation into body substances and feces. This raises the question: at what point – and for how long – is the object identifiable as such? To what extent does the classification of something as a certain kind of food include the phases before and after the ideal state of the finished – and intact – product? Is raw dough already considered a croissant? Generally speaking, the individual ingredients are not yet recognized as the dish in question, yet a shaped but still raw croissant is already considered a croissant. Before and after its idealized state, a meal is just like any other object – it is the defined object as long as it is recognized as such. With food, however, this period is particularly short-lived due to it being consumed during use, and because food goes off. The following discussion and analysis always starts off from the item's ideal condition rather than its true physical condition. Items in a less-than-ideal condition are not encouraged either, they are rejected; presumably so as not to tarnish the image of the ideal condition but to preserve it as strictly as possible. Such items are shown in photographs or films only rarely; discussed or shown only in the most clandestine circles. Food in a pre-use condition (sometimes even before that: live animals, raw meat and fish) are sometimes even considered taboo or disgusting.

Dishes as artifacts – Goulash, for example

Every recipe is in principle a design instruction. Every hamburger, every pizza and every chocolate cake is a product created according to certain rules (which, of course, are constantly evolving over time) and is perceived as such by a given community. It would be possible to do an empirical study of the very characteristics that make a croissant a croissant, a sushi a sushi or a curry a curry. Of course, design objects are never clearly differentiated as concepts (neither are linguistic objects), but nevertheless a combination of core features leads to a certain group of people perceiving these dishes as such.

The essence of the concept of "goulash," an attempt to describe it

What makes a goulash a goulash? It is the use of the basic ingredients onion, meat and paprika, the creamy consistency of the sauce, the finely cut pieces of meat and the dark red color. Conversely, this means a yellow, blue or green goulash is not a goulash. A goulash is not goulash if the sauce is too runny or the meat is served whole. The situation is different when it comes to the basic ingredients, however, because there is such a thing as a tofu goulash, or a goulash without meat; there is a pumpkin goulash, a bean goulash, etc.
So what is it that makes a goulash a goulash? If the exclusion principle is to be followed, a goulash ultimately boils down to this definition: a savory stew with a thick sauce and small chunks of a single main ingredient. Of course, the "filler" – or the meat, tofu or pumpkin – shouldn't be cut either too small (for example, chopped), or too large. A survey could be conducted among goulash-eaters to narrow down the range of acceptable dimensions and proportions for pieces of meat in goulash in order to make it a proper goulash. A paprika schnitzel is truly not a goulash, but then neither is a chili con carne called a goulash. In the both cases, because the meat contained is too large or too small or not proportioned correctly, and in the second the sauce contains other, non-pureed ingredients such as slices of red pepper or beans. So if you try to extract the essence of goulash, it all comes down to the way the main ingredient is shredded and its size and texture ratio to the surrounding sauce, which must be red and contain paprika.

Convention and the issue of time

It is not just the physical item that goes through a process of change over the course of its existence; the content which the item conveys as a symbol also continuously mutates. As mentioned earlier, the meaning of food items is regionally, situationally and context-dependent, but also changes over time. "The sign refers not only to actual possibilities of human action, but also to a complexity of issues evolving through time by virtue of the interpretative act. A string of signs evolves."[90] Signs emerge by convention; i.e., they develop over time and are constantly changing. Their message depends on the recipient group – those people who recognize and can decipher the sign, who are themselves constantly changing. How content and form relate to a specific sign depends on region and time period. The same shape can mean something different in different places and/ or at different times. Signs are neither general nor everlasting, but are use- and situation-dependent.[91] The meaning of signs, in this case the specific meaning of food items, changes constantly through its use.

The shift in the meaning of a culinary object over time can be demonstrated, for example, by the croissant. In antiquity, croissants were a bread offering that represented the crescent moon.[92] "There can be little doubt over what the croissant represents, given the old name 'panes lunati' – moon bread – from a Carolingian monastic text (St. Gallen) [...] the croissant turns out to be a moon symbol."[93] The croissant was originally a pre-Christian pastry offering, the shape of which had strong symbolic-mythological value.[94] The moon, with its cyclically recurring phases, stands as a symbol of fertility and growth among others, and is often represented in the form of horns, especially bull horns.[95] In early Christianity, croissants were also used as eucharistic bread because the curved sickle of the waxing moon after the darkness of the new moon was interpreted as a symbol of the risen Christ.[96] Later, the association of the shape with devil's horns – which can still be found today in the German name for croissants, "Hörnchen" (small horn) – was adopted in Europe. It is also possible from a mythological perspective to establish a connection between the moon symbol and the devil's horns: The moon goddess Semele's son – begotten by Zeus – was Dionysus, the Greek god of inebriation and transgression. In Christianity, he mutated into the devil. "Dionysus also wore horns that showed he was the son of a moon goddess."[97]

In order to recognize and evaluate any object it first needs to be interpreted. Since food products are three-dimensional objects, their perception and interpretation are more complex than, say, language or text, since all five senses are involved and interact accordingly with each other. The particular status of foods within the category of things, namely that they are consumed and are therefore also perceived inside the body, complicates the analysis of culinary perception and interpretation still further. Hence, food products are complex compositions that are hard to read and even harder to describe.[98] The perception of sensory stimuli is a cognitive-emotional process. Perception and recognition are not possible without classification. People can perceive nothing other than by means of sign systems, which act as classification systems[99] and connect the symbolic (emblematic, idealized) content of an object to its sensory experience conveyed via corresponding stimuli. The "shapes" or "forms" sifted from the incoming sensory data are classified into an already existing system of (linguistic) concepts or non-verbal meanings. "That which all adequate conceptions of an object must have in common, is the concept of the object. The same concept is embodied in a multitude of conceptions. It is a form that appears in all versions of thought or imagery that can connote the object in question [...]"[100] This association already contains modes of behavior and issues instructions for use. Because the kind of association which aids perception is man-made and learned, it can be referred to as modifiable. This type of perception can therefore be re-learned and reshaped, but also exploited.

The basic tendency to arrange sensory impressions into groups and patterns forms the basis for abstraction and rationality.[101] Without them, we would neither be able to perceive nor think. Conceptual systems enable the building of this construct of ideas, which creates orderly, spatio-temporal reality. They constitute a purely mental world of ideas, which serves as a reference system for experience and the processing of sensory impulses. "A concept is all that a symbol really conveys."[102]

In the case of food, one of the primary classification systems is the contrast between the two basic tastes "sweet" and "savory." Other principles classify food according to its ingredients or its order of consumption; e.g., whether it is a starter, a main course, a dessert, a snack or a drink. From this perspective, the five basic tastes of sweet, sour, salty, bitter and umami can also be interpreted as a (linguistic) repertoire in the form of a taste code which provides information about how food is to be used, thus guiding the behavior of the eater. In the case of "sweet" and "savory" for example, this being when and how to combine and eat something. The categories "main course," "starter," "dessert" etc. also work in a similar way, even if the coding is not always as clear as with the basic types of taste. Other classification criteria for food products are their function, e.g., nutritional supplements; texture (soup, cream, jelly, cake, drink, smoothie, etc. which in this case acts as a sign for a particular category of food); as well as the overall dietary category: a healthy diet, a low-fat diet, etc.

One place in which culinary patterns of classification are demonstrated is supermarkets, where food and other things are arranged into categories such as basic foods and ingredients (vegetables, bread, sausage, etc.), preservatives (canned foods, jam, frozen foods), physical state (drinks, frozen products), cultural origin, mealtimes (breakfast, snack, etc.) or processed (canned, ready meals). The classification criteria mean that some levels of meaning the goods contain are emphasized by their arrangement, while others are relegated into the background. Associations that are encouraged include certain combinations of ingredients – the components of a sandwich are often next to each other – or recipes (from sugar sprinkles to baking soda and marzipan roses; everything that is necessary for baking a cake is placed next to the flour). In principle, how food items are arranged in supermarkets amounts to user instructions for how they are to be further used; in other words how they are to be processed and/or consumed afterwards. Calories and nutritional value e.g. on the other hand become less significant in comparison to e.g., media publications about food. Were the food products in a supermarket to be arranged according to different criteria which would seem quite normal in other contexts – e.g., according to price, nutritional value, consistency, size and shape, weight or color – we may very well discover at the checkout that different things had ended up in the shopping cart, since such arrangement criteria could convey different information and presumably lead to different buying habits.

The selection of food as a sign

Food is – with a few exceptions – culturally rather than biologically defined. Its biological makeup alone does not necessarily tell people what they should eat – and what not. Countless culturally influenced decisions take place between feeling the physiological craving of "hunger" or "thirst" and satisfying it by eating or drinking. People predominantly satisfy their biological requirements in a culturally relevant fashion; e.g., through traditions.[103] The range of foods that are biologically eligible is constrained by social and cultural rules determining the selection, processing and consumption of food. In extreme cases, this culinary classification can even completely override the nutritional urgings of human biology: "The breaking of taboos on human flesh or other forbidden foods sometimes seemed worse than physical death."[104]

In some respects, all items are in a certain sense "implanted" through socio-cultural categorization into "food products" or "non-food products" from the outset, and this message or content is then in turn received when the previously defined item is consumed. Since the division of the environment into "edible" and "inedible" is already a classification and an evaluation, every piece of food is a sign per se. Food products, if they are recognized as such, at least have the meaning of being edible in any case. Moreover, the vast majority of food products are deliberately altered in some way prior to consumption; in other words, they are designed (by breeding, processing, preparation, mincing, etc.) and thus also signal the kind of needs they have been adapted to. The distinction between "edible" and "inedible" creates a culture-dependent, regional system of signs that translates the moral organization of a society "into practical, instantly applicable instructions for use."[105] This symbolic function that comestibles have applies to ritual culinary rules and taboos as much as to food selection in modern consumer society – keyword health, low fat, fair trade, etc. – as a means to implement moral, social, ethical, etc. values or abstract concepts from other areas of life. As a result, membership of a particular group for instance – whether it be social class, age group, gender, political affiliation, religion or other communities – is also expressed through the selection and rejection of certain foods, meals and drinks.[106]

Diets – that is, the compilation of a certain range of foods – refer to codes that serve to socially stratify and differentiate, thus making determinations "about belonging or not belonging to a social group or culture."[107] The symbolism of the chosen range of food, however, goes beyond simple group affiliation, even if it is not consciously observed by all members, and many people (at least superficially) only decide for or against a dish, a food or an ingredient by convention. The verdict of "edible" or "inedible" is based on very specific criteria that reflect a very specific life plan. When Freegans dine exclusively on discarded food, they are using their choice of what to eat as a form of political activism to express their criticisms of capitalism, consumerism and the throwaway society etc.; and to advocate for a different social model (e.g., alternative economic models) in a radical manner.

Meanings that are generally associated with objects – food, in this case – also relate to higher-level values beyond the world of food: e.g., socio-political motives in the case of vegetarianism; connection to a higher-level, divine plane in the case of religious taboos; criticism of the system in the case of Freeganism. People partly express their worldview through their culinary selection criteria. Vegetarians, vegans or people who refrain from certain types of meat, or those who eat low-fat or sugar-free foods, make their own taboos in terms of food intake and voluntarily place physical non-essential restrictions upon themselves. The given choice follows a moral code that doesn't necessarily have to be religiously motivated but makes sense to those in question, not only in terms of belonging to a community but also in the implementation of ideas and concepts that have nothing to do with nutrition.

Roland Barthes, for example, describes that the attitude towards sugar is not just a question of nutrition, but also a kind of motto for life: "Sugar is not just one – albeit common – food; it is, if you like, an 'attitude'; it is bound to customs, to 'protocols' that are no longer determined solely by nutrition."[108] To eat something that has been richly sweetened means "to experience the day, the rest, the journey and the idleness in a certain way through the sugar."[109] Sugar – just like "sugar-free" – is an institution that contains images, dreams, taboos, inclinations, predilections and values.[110]

The symbolism of meat

If supporters of vegetarianism deliberately give up a certain basic ingredient, be it for religious, moral, political or hierarchical motives, they are giving out a strong social signal: anyone who doesn't eat meat automatically renounces all symbolism associated with this basic ingredient.[111]

Why do vegetarians reject meat, of all things? Could they achieve the same symbolic effect by not eating bread? A social differentiation from other groups would probably work with bread – but a socio-political one probably wouldn't. The symbolism of vegetarianism is best examined through the symbolism of the flesh, since meat is not just a type of food; the eating of it is also a lifestyle.[112] According to Scottish social anthropologist Nick Fiddes, eating meat is "an expression of those same core values of modern western society: of power, of superiority [...] of civilization."[113]

When meat was obtained by hunting big game, wild animals were not only a food source but also a deadly threat. Eating meat not only meant hunting, but also being hunted at the same time; securing meat was a life-threatening activity.[114] Meat thus clearly and directly represented "a potent symbol of power over the wilderness."[115] In the mind of the hunters, once a large animal had been brought down, its powers and strengths were transferred to the eaters by consuming the meat. The transferal of a large, mighty animal's physical characteristics via its incorporation (especially certain innards such as the heart, brain or kidneys) is a common theme in mythology and superstition. "Meat satisfies our bodies but it also feeds our minds. We eat not only the animal's flesh; with it we drain their lifeblood and so seize their strength [...]; consuming its flesh is a statement that we are the unquestioned masters of the world."[116] To this day, meat is a symbol of strength. "Meat was, and remains, a venerable symbol of potency, and indeed of civilization itself."[117]

The consumption of meat is said to bestow strength, the symbolic effect in recent times being more from lean meat – especially when (partially) bloody[118] – than from the innards.[119] The symbolism of the strengthening effect of meat, for example, served as a slogan for advertising "Daonino," a cream cheese product from the French food manufacturer Danone containing fruits, which claims that Daonino have the same value as a small steak. For Barthes in France in the 1950s, a steak symbolized the transition of an animal's strength into food: "The beef steak belongs to the same blood mythology as wine. It is the heart of the flesh [...] whoever takes it is assimilating bovine strength."[120]

In Western culture, the raw material "meat" is one of the most symbolically loaded ingredients. Whoever consumes meat has power over the lives of others. "Killing, cooking, and eating other animal's flesh provides perhaps the ultimate authentication of human superiority over the rest of nature."[121] Meat comes from dead animals – the fundamental conflict of human existence; having to eat other living things or parts of them in order to survive is most starkly obvious with meat. Meat is thus at the interface between positive (own survival) and negative (danger, killing) – value systems. In many cultures, the transfer of the slaughtered animal from one system to the other is accomplished by means of magic: The transformation of the material "meat" from the body of an animal into food is expressed in the ritualization of slaughter and in animal sacrifice.[122]

"In Greek social and religious thought, the consumption of meat and the enactment of blood-related sacrificial rituals were directly related."[123] Slaughter was associated with the respective sacrificial rituals that were performed by priests. While the daily cooking was a woman's business in ancient Greece, the preparation of meat dishes was the responsibility of the men. The so-called "mágheiros," a term whose root word can still be recognized in the word "magician," but also in the Italian word "macelleria" (butcher shop) or the German word "Metzger" (butcher), was a combination of sacrificial priest and chef all rolled into one person. Originally, the chef practiced ritual functions above all else; namely the transferring of the dead animal into the kitchen and into food.[124]

Meat plays a central role in both Jewish and Christian religions, whether in the form of animal sacrifices, slaughter rituals or fasting.[125] To this day, meat as a base culinary material occupies a special position in the kitchen, and is strongly associated with moral debates. "The eating of meat is the main element of modern food culture, which manifests itself as a democratized form of the Greek sacrificial meal, the constitutive act of the polity."[126] The range of meat that is for eating is very small compared to the range of potentially consumable organisms available. This small number of species is virtually taboo-free; dead animals that can be positively reinterpreted as meat. We recoil from all other dead animals. Meat is strongly perceived with disgust while it is being prepared (for example, in the kitchen); even

on the plate, an impression of disgust can quickly replace that of pleasure if color, consistency or smell don't quite meet expectations.
Meat, with its ambivalence between our own life and other life,
represents an unsolvable dilemma that can only be tackled on a
religious or moral level. This conflicting attitude towards meat
as a dead animal is also evident in the design of meat dishes. A
dissociation from the dead carcass takes place, among other things
through an appropriately robust processing and/or abstract design of
the original product: Certain preparation methods such as chopping,
blending and mincing alter the basic ingredient "meat" beyond
recognition. Compositions such as spam, pork pies, sausages and
meatloaf satisfy the need to free meat from the experience of its
typical characteristics such as gristle, skin, bones, etc., and transform
it into a uniform, homogeneous mass. As a homogeneous, soft, pink
slice of sausage, meat has completely lost its natural appearance.[127]
This creative disguising "erases" traditional meat symbolism (in a
manner quite comparable to sacrificial and slaughter rituals), at the
same time turning the symbolic value scale back to zero. A new,
different, virginal and harmless product is created via this process:
finely blended sausages, meatballs, hamburgers, fish fingers etc.,
which in turn also lose their "power": Pork sausage, hamburger and
chicken nuggets do not make one "strong," but "fat." The message
of these foods has changed from powerful meat to "childish," "soft"
and "unhealthy": also in old ideas, like the fantastical land of plenty
sausages don't inspire strength but fatigue.

Food Design: Processing and preparation (designing) as sign-making and knowledge transfer

Humans transform their environment to suit their needs. The process
of this transformation is called design; its outcome is the design
product. Just like all other everyday objects, be they tools, furniture,
means of transport or clothing, the majority of foods are subject to

this transformation process. Because food is a physical item, it always has an appearance and therefore a corresponding object language, whether this is perceived consciously or unconsciously by the eater: There is no food without form. When this form is perceived, it is collated with culturally learned patterns of meaning in the brain. The sorting into this pattern of meaning is what lends significance to any form. Since object language – in contrast to verbal language – does not have clearly defined units of meaning (words), the content is always linked to the form; every form always automatically means "something."[128] This means that no food is free of meaning. The design of the food always makes a statement, because even when people are obtaining their food from pristine nature, they have learned to locate it and recognize it as food, i.e., as having a certain meaning.

When people influence the design of a food, we are referring to an edible design object which is created in a corresponding design process, that of food design. The decisions that are made in the course of such design processes are individual in nature, but come from within a network of cultural motives, rules and customs. Just as the selection of what counts as food is a group-made socio-political decision, so too is the design of food prescribed by the group within a cultural framework. It is no accident that a specific food culture is an essential part of a society. If one thinks of culture as a system of meanings,[129] then food and its design is a means of expressing this system. It makes no difference whether food is prepared in the kitchen, ordered in the restaurant or bought in the supermarket; every person actively chooses a certain type of design before every meal. Which forms of design are favored – i.e., consumed – and which are rejected depends on the structure of meaning – to which individual members on the whole defer with little hesitation – the culture in question has. At the end of the day, we don't eat what we personally like, but rather those items that fit into the culturally prescribed system of meaning with which we identify, i.e., those that have the "right" meaning. This is because strictly speaking, a socialized person cannot have a purely "individual" taste, as the perception of sensory taste signals is culturally shaped as such.

Every (seemingly) mundane, everyday commodity, be it a chewing gum, a frozen pizza, an ice lolly or ketchup, contains a meaning that goes beyond the mere provision of nutrients. The dualistic nature of functional use-value on the one hand and its aesthetic-symbolic meaning on the other applies to every single tiny, insignificant thing[130] – even a stock cube. The relationship between the actual function (of the food) and the aesthetic-symbolic added value is of particular significance in the case of food, because even taste is an (aesthetic) surplus value that isn't actually necessary for nutrition. Tasteless food (if it hasn't gone off) does its job just as well as food that tastes good. Of course, under certain circumstances people do or did have to eat things that do not taste good just to satisfy their hunger. Even today in the western world, we tend to do this more often than we are aware: take convenience food, fast food, sandwiches or some of the etiquette involved in eating as a guest. By far the most important function of the vast majority of items is neither their use value nor their practical-technical functions, but their aesthetic-symbolic qualities.[131]

The success or failure (in the cultural sense) of an object is ultimately determined by the signs that it gives off and not by whether or not it works. In extreme cases, the dominance of symbolic factors extends to objects which are primarily to be experienced, and are only carriers of meaning without having any (practical) function. We could point to works of art if we are talking about non-edible objects,[132] or in the case of food there are also dishes that contain virtually no calories, i.e., that have no practical value. The (sugarless) chewing gum, for example, provides the eater with a sensory experience, but contains no energy. When it comes to the question of whether or not we will put something in our mouth, symbolic quality is the determining factor. With many foods, nutritional value and practical functions such as shelf life, preparation time, palatability, etc. take a back seat over symbolic meaning; even aesthetic qualities like taste become secondary if the message is on point. One example is the principal ritual food for Christians, the communion wafer. When it is eaten, taste and nutritional value are irrelevant. Although the central ritual of holy communion is the faithful's incorporation of the divine, that is eating the body of Christ; though in fact Jesus is really a wafer with an abstract geometrical shape – the appearance of which is more reminiscent of a round piece of cardboard than of bread – that is being stuck in the mouth. The design of the wafer, however, with its bite-sized pre-portioning and long shelf life, is quite functional, and of course also conveys certain symbolic content due to its round shape. There is also the Tic-tac, which is advertised as having only two calories, much like Coke Zero. These are not necessarily consumed because of their use value (i.e., to satisfy hunger or thirst) but primarily because of their symbolic value, and are strictly speaking not actually "foods," but "edible items" – objects that are incorporated for reasons other than feeding the body.

Display food: a contradiction in terms

The symbolic quality of food is particularly evident in dishes that are never intended to be eaten. Food products which have been relieved of their very purpose of keeping the body alive and thus of their use value, act as pure carriers of meaning. They are prepared for the sole purpose of communicating a message or some content. "Food" that is not for eating is actually a contradiction in terms, yet it has for centuries been a permanent fixture in certain menus and cookbooks.[133] During the Renaissance, so-called "trionfi" were a common sight – magnificent table sculptures made of sugar, marzipan, butter or dough which served as nothing more than a decoration, and thus had no practical use. In 1509, for example, the "Sacrifice of Isaac" – a scene made of wax, linen and wood together with a marzipan tower – was depicted as a separate course between cabbage and fish brine at the funeral feast of the Bavarian Duke Albrecht IV.[134] Table sculptures portrayed mythological scenes such as the horse Pegasus, reproductions of nature such as trees bearing fruits, allegories and even exotic animals like elephants.[135] In 1650, German poet Georg Philipp Harsdörffer made an explicit distinction between edible display food and non-edible display dishes that were only meant for show in one of his texts. Even in Johannes Georg Krünitz's economic-technological encyclopedia in 1825, the keyword "Schauessen" (display food) reveals food that was only put on the table for decoration together with the other dishes, but that always remained untouched.[136] The phenomenon of display food is known even today – for example as "finely garnished" plate-edge decorations in the form of lemon slices, basil or sprigs of parsley. Other examples of contemporary display food are: cake decorations made from wafers; sugar or marzipan which are often not eaten; orange, lemon, cucumber or other fruit and vegetable slices on cocktail sticks and mixed drinks; or dishes such as glazed pig's head, which are only presented as a decoration in buffets.[137] Also to be found next to pieces of meat and side dishes are individual lettuce leaves or dried tomato slices, which are intended for visual – but not actual – consumption only. These items work through the senses purely remotely – mostly visually, but sometimes via the sense of smell, such as herbal decorations: A sprig of rosemary on grilled meat signifies freshness. Such items act as signs to enhance the food next to them and to communicate its freshness. A bit like underlined or bold text in writing, the decoration at the edge of your plate that is not intended for consumption enhances the value of the food it is placed next to.

Edible items act as sign carriers. When the decision as to what is "edible" and what is not is first made, i.e., the question of choosing basic products is settled, a large number of further decisions have to be made: how to process them, removal of unwanted components (peeling, removing gristle, bones, tendons, offal, etc.), type of preparation, portion size, distribution on the plate and so on needs to be determined. After the initial decision in the course of the meal is made, namely that of its contents, hundreds more follow. How they are decided is what determines the design of the finished dish or meal. The design of the item "food," e.g., the way bread, noodles or biscuits are made, influences the qualities the food item has and is thus the starting point for the symbolism of food.

The reasons for which food design choices are made (or for buying specifically designed food products) reflect a group's cultural structure of meaning: the way food is designed (or which designs are purchased) indicates which meanings are associated with or projected onto the food in a given cultural environment. If "culture" is understood as being "the result of a process of negotiating meaning between culturally influenced individuals who are nevertheless capable of reflection and innovation,"[138] then this group-specific network of meaning forms the framework conditions (constraints, restrictions) for the design of food. Culture as an open – i.e., changeable and designable – symbolic code sets out the limitations and conditions according to which designers (or buyers) work (decide), and in this way confer (or select, accept, and thus indirectly shape) a certain shape (appearance) to the food products – consciously or unconsciously, intentionally or accidentally – and thereby a certain symbolism. Swiss social anthropologist Andreas Wimmer calls it the "social dynamics of the production of purpose"[139] and also talks about a "process of producing meaning."[140] However, food is not merely the sum of the decisions (motivations) made regarding its consumption, but fully-fledged signs that can be considered elements of their own communication system: "This means that it [food] is not only a feature of a complex of more-or-less conscious motivations, but an outright sign, or perhaps even the functioning unit of a communication structure."[141]

Deconstruction into individual components: Properties as sign carriers

To analyze the semantic dimension of objects, Susann Vihma formulates two central questions:

1. What do the reference relations represent when they are interpreted?
2. How are the contents represented?[142]

Applied to the analysis of food products as sign vehicles, this means: what contents communicate culinary signs, and how are these conveyed?

Problems with the (discursive) description

The attempt to describe technical symbols in more detail is actually doomed to failure, because while in conventional language all meanings must be exclusively conveyed in sequence and must be grasped one at a time, the symbols of design language can only be understood instantly, simultaneously and holistically.[143] A discursive description of material signs therefore automatically involves a certain loss of meaning and is as such subject to a certain degree of inaccuracy and vagueness. These translations provide at best only analogies, and are more or less automatically susceptible to uncertainty.[144] In some cases, therefore, in order to describe or clarify the effect and functionality of a sign it appears more appropriate to translate it into another kind of object or visual language, e.g., photographs.

Attempting the impossible

All these considerations aside, we would still like to try to analyze and describe the symbolism of food linguistically. First of all, it must be stressed that not only food products in the form of entire dishes such as hamburger or pizza and in the form of diets such as vegetarianism or kosher food act as signs. A dish such as steak and chips also contains several individual elements, each of which are in turn significant. Just as whether an armchair is made of wood, metal, plastic or paper influences its use and its meaning, the fact that fries – with which certain meanings are already linked – are made of potato also contributes to the overall concept "steak and chips." Food not only acts as a sign on the level of entire products, but also on those of individual product properties: "It can thus be seen [...] that the meaning [...] does not capture the different types of products, but only the flavors: the delicate and the bitter are in significant opposition."[145] According to Barthes, these specific product properties form "units" of the food system, as do "dry," "creamy," "watery," "sweet" and "crispy."[146]

Just like language itself, object language has its own compound forms. Every object can basically be divided into subordinate subcomponents, which have their own meanings. With food, all properties (smell, sound, material, shape, etc.) are relevant in this context given that they are potential "units" with symbolic characteristics, as is social use: i.e., how the object is dealt with, e.g.,the production or the operation. Each three-dimensional object has to contain the elements of form (geometry in space) and materiality. Every form must be of a given material. Conversely, there can be no material without form. As a result of objects being perceived via the five senses, every object – whether edible or not always has a color, a sound (type of acoustic feedback) and feel (haptic impression) quality, a smell and a taste.

To strip an object down into its individual components that carry meaning in the sense of design language is clearly more complicated than it is with conventional language, since basically every attribute, every tiniest little feature, comes into question as a potential meaning carrier. Not only can color itself be meaningful, but also individual shades, color gradients, color changes and highlights. Likewise, not only can a shape as a whole make a statement, but so can individual parts such as hollows, grooves, creases, ridges, openings or joins. The type and number of units is far more complex than with classical language, and doesn't follow any (obvious) system. To make matters worse, individual levels of meaning also interact with each other; in other words, meaning can come about by the interaction of visual and acoustic characteristics, for instance. While a sentence can, practically speaking, consist only of words, an object can be split into a seemingly infinite and endlessly diverse number of meaningful entities until finally one arrives at units that are no longer meaningful, e.g., individual notches, curves, points, sounds, etc., which – in a similar way to individual syllables or letters of the language – no longer make sense without reference to the overall system. The number of subordinate symbolic layers that can be brought to light depends not only on the complexity of the object (as a symbol), but also on perspective, i.e., by the interpreter and interpretive tool being used (the eyes, for instance).

In addition, the association of a meaning to an element in object language is flexible and varies according to context: therefore, a clear definition of the elements and their content is impossible. A sub-element can communicate different, even contrary meanings in another configuration or to those of the object per se, depending on context. Thus, the color brown for example may stand for "crunchy crust," "spoiled fruit" or "roasted." Nevertheless, the element "brown" in each of these meaning relationships remains significant: a brown apple means something different from a green one; a beige bread crust something other than a dark brown one, etc.

One example of the relativity of what the color black means being dependent upon context (specifically the context of taste) can be seen in Coca-Cola. Significant features of Coca-Cola include its reddish brown, almost black color, its opacity and its carbon dioxide, so that the bubbles are only partly visible when being poured. The specific way it refracts light, its extremely sweet taste and its tingling-sticky mouthfeel are further typical factors. In food, black usually signifies a bitter taste, warns against spoiled or toxic substances, and is often associated with rejection or disgust.[147] However, when combined with an extremely sweet taste – a rather rare combination in nature (one example would be blackberries) – it changes the perception of the color: as soon as one overcomes the psychological inhibition against consuming the opaque, black liquid, a surprisingly sweet taste follows. The interplay between the contradictory characteristics of the culinary perception of "black" and "extreme sweetness" provides the drink a unique selling point. Coca-Cola isn't comparable to other drinks because it has the contradictory, sensory qualities "opaque-sparkling" (something happening on the inside that you do not see before, but only feel in your mouth) and "black-sweet," and is therefore not easy to classify. It has a special sensory status that creates a mysterious aura, a magical or ritualistic image.

As the example of Cola shows, the individual levels of meaning influence each other – both within the perception of each individual sense, but also as the various sensory perceptions in combination with each other. The way in which the taste components of individual ingredients in a finished dish, for example, form a distinctive taste can be compared with the process of mixing color: in a similar way to different colors, the different flavors like "sweet," "salty," "bitter," "lemony," "creamy," "chocolaty" etc. can be mixed, and can then intensify, supplement, suppress, cancel out or even reverse each other's effects. Sweet and sour, for example, intensify each other at low concentrations and suppress each other or have no effect at high concentrations. Sour and bitter intensify each other at low concentrations; at medium amounts, sour suppresses bitter, whereas at high concentrations, a sour taste is toned down by bitter ingredients. Sweet and salty intensify each other at low concentrations and weaken each other at high levels. In addition, the perception of sweetness is temperature-dependent.[148] Sweet also decreases spicy; spicy suppresses sour, sweet, bitter and umami.[149] Moreover, there are substances – four are known so far – that qualitatively change taste. The West African miracle fruit (Synsepalum dulcificum) contains miraculine, which for example apparently turns from sour-tasting into sweet upon eating.[150]

The mélange of all nuances of taste and their meanings ultimately creates the "actual" taste of a dish, in which all meaningful individual components of the item interact with each other. In the putting together of a certain arrangement – be it a sandwich, a curry or an ice-cream – a new level of meaning emerges: that of the whole object. In certain circumstances, individual ingredients or characteristics are no longer (consciously) perceivable, yet they influence the overall experience and contribute to the taste of the food or to the meaning of the object. It is impossible to predict how the individual components in the overall object will fit together, so an examination on a case-by-case basis is needed.

Individual components (units/properties) and how they transmit meanings: Examples

The attempt to "read" food objects in the sense of design language – i.e., to separate them into individual components and filter out which meanings are linked to them, how they work for themselves and in relation to the total object (composition) – must be done individually for each object. The result cannot be generalized and unfortunately does not offer any conclusions about the functioning of other signs. The following case studies are therefore not a systematic analysis, merely a few examples of how the aesthetic features of food can transmit meaning.

Shape, Example 1: The cake slice

Generally shapes seem to have an effect on the expected taste: rounder shapes for examples tend to be perceived as sweeter and creamier compared to objects with sharper edges; when a producer rounded off the corners of a well-known chocolate bar consumers had the impression that it tasted sweeter and creamier even though the recipe had not been changed.[151]

The notion that specific shapes can convey certain associations can be demonstrated e.g., in the case of a triangular piece of cake: Food in the shape of a triangle is actually rather unusual: psychologically because it always has an acute angle pointing at the consumer; ergonomically (especially with small objects such as chocolates) because it fits poorly into the mouth; and technically because (industrially) triangles are not easy to produce, stack and package. One exception is the Toblerone, for example: it uses its triangular shape as a unique selling point, and the problem of stackability is solved by having a cross-section the shape of an equilateral triangle, which can be tessellated together perfectly. In traditional food products, a triangular shape often comes about by halving or folding a square or rectangle, e.g., with ravioli or in the case of triangular sandwiches, which are produced by cutting diagonally across sandwiched slices of toasting bread. In this case, the triangle is actually a further processed (or divided) square.

The cake slice – a jutting, pointed triangle with a curved outer edge, is also associated with a specific type of division. The circular shape of the whole cake – representing unity, completeness, geometric perfection, flawlessness, community and belonging among other things – stands in contrast to the triangular, single cake slice. Composed of valuable and special ingredients, a cake becomes a festival dish that marks special occasions (for example, birthdays, weddings). The way it is always divided – invariably through the middle into triangular cake slices – and who gets to do it reflects the hierarchies within the group according to the occasion: everyone gets an equal-sized piece (there is no best slice for the patriarch, unlike what is customary for a roast). The division of food is not undertaken by the highest-ranking person in the hierarchy; it is those who are the focus of the ceremony that cut the cake: The bride and groom (and always together – if one were to do it alone, that would be deemed bad luck) or the birthday boy/girl. This is even the case with 3-year-olds, to whom one would never give a big knife under normal circumstances. The festive expression of the circular shape, which is without direction and non-hierarchical, is reflected in the way in which a round cake is consumed.

Cutting by halving, quartering, into eighths and so forth through the middle is a basic function with cakes (and other round dishes that are eaten all at once), as it guarantees that each person receives an equal piece of equal value (in proportion of edge and main body). Portioning rituals determine the shape and symbolism of food. While the shape of bread slices doesn't have any special meaning because it results from the ongoing portioning of a daily meal, other kinds of slices are symbolically loaded. A food product in the form of a wedge of cake is interpreted as the outcome of a (fair) division and is thus understood as part of a larger whole, even if a division may have never actually taken place. Cake slice-shaped food, whatever it is made of, represents a single portion within a group of like items; an association the specific shape of which is transferred to other types of products, e.g., pre-packed wafers or pre-portioned cheese. As cheese triangles are made of soft cheese which is melted hard cheese, cheese spreads can generally be made into a variety of shapes. The triangular shape of the "cheese triangle" is technically not mandatory, but is freely chosen. The small foil-wrapped triangles made of soft cheese suggest that they belong to a larger whole; they give the impression of having been part of a large cheese wheel and of being the result of a traditional method of production, although they are actually produced in different ways.[152]

Shape, Example 2: The fish finger

The cuboid shape of the fish finger, or the combination of the shape "cuboid" with the material "fish," clearly indicates that this is a highly processed, industrially manufactured food. Whereas the design of other products masks the fact that they are mass-produced, e.g., imitating the shape of a hand-made product (for example, for rolls made with the bread machine), the shape of the fish finger blatantly flaunts its artificiality and industrial manufacture. If fish is frozen into blocks, then cut into unrealistic, equally proportioned, uniform rectangles, it no longer seems like fish. With their building-block angularity, the design of fish fingers causes them to be disassociated from fish; indeed, with their geometric form they are likely to be seen as "non-fish." Their strict geometric shape disguises the basic product in such a way that it gives no hint of its composition; the raw material remains abstract. (Which in the case of the fish finger is part of the idea. The raw substance "fish" is neither shown on the packaging nor in commercials.) The technical abstraction from the raw product leads to a complete change in appearance and aroma: Finished fish fingers are visually no longer reminiscent of fish in terms of taste and texture. The cuboid shape is not only functional – having manufacturing advantages and being stackable – but the geometric shape's symbolism also serves to reassure all those who, for whatever reason, do not want to think about the fact that they are eating fish.

With food, angular, geometric shapes like cuboids often denote "artificiality" in the sense of a strong cultural transformation of food because in nature there is – except salt – no ingredient that would be rectangular from its origin. Processing, however, does not necessarily have to be industrial. A rectangular shape can also be the result of a traditional preparation process and thus have the connotation of "artificial" but not of "industrial"; e.g., Sashimi, raw pieces of fish that are traditionally cut perfectly rectangular in Japan.

Shape, Example 3: The Croissant

Of course, as is the case with many other items, specific shapes are also used as an essential feature that signifies a certain type of food. Croissants are a type of bakery product the name of which refers to neither a specific recipe nor to a taste, but only to the external shape and the main ingredient, flour. A croissant can be an almond croissant, a butter croissant, a custard croissant, a chocolate croissant or any number of savory croissants among others. All these food products are of varying sizes, different tastes and are eaten on different occasions. The only thing they have in common is the fact that they are all baked products and that they have a curved, horseshoe or crescent shape. The specific physical shape is the essential feature of a croissant and acts as a variety denomination or to make the term "croissant" distinctive.

Material/Ingredients

As is the case with other everyday items – what a drinking vessel, for instance, is used for depends on whether it is made of paper, glass or metal (e.g., ritual vessels or sports trophies) – food is also judged according to its raw materials. Whether the filling between the two halves of a sandwich is of meat or fish changes the meaning of the finished meal. If the classic hamburger draws heavily upon meat symbolism, then the fish burger is automatically attached to the ideas and values associated with the material "fish."

Material/Ingredients, Example 1: Sugar

Materials possess character, i.e., they act as signs. In the form of coarse sugar or a thin coating of icing sugar, the material "sugar" on brioche braids, Bundt cakes, donuts or other pastry dishes acts as a mark of quality that symbolizes luxury and taste, despite superficially being "merely" a decoration that makes desserts look "nicer." However, even if it were only for optical effect, cakes could be sprinkled with corn starch or flour, as is done with bread, for example. (Flour is also a main ingredient of cakes and pastries, but it doesn't convey the symbolic message of sweetness and tastiness in order to function as a cake decoration.) In fact, sugar on pastries is a visual sign indicating that they contain a lot of sugar inside. It implies a sweet taste, which is why it seems so appetizing – not only on the level of the senses but also mentally: sugar symbolically relaxes and soothes, making one feel very bountiful, indeed opulent, in a situation where there must clearly be more than enough to go round. This aura of contentment, fullness, freedom from fear and cares is also associated, for example, with very sweet drinks. Signs are always dependent on situation, time and context, however – so sugar has negative connotations in other contexts precisely because of what it means and is deliberately avoided as a substance in certain foods, e.g., Cola Zero.

Material/Ingredients, Example 2: Chocolate, granola and milky bars

Even the selection of the main ingredient is a question of design. The mere decision to cook fish or meat makes a different statement. Just as a table is afforded a different quality on account of whether it is made of wood, glass or steel, a snack bar also changes its meaning depending on whether it consists primarily of chocolate, granola or milk. Certain ascriptions are inherent in different materials per se; or to put it the other way round, materials work as symbols, too. Just as a spoon is perceived differently depending on whether it is made of plastic or steel, the material "granola" also transforms a snack bar into a "granola bar," to which completely different ideas are associated than, say, are with a chocolate bar: even though shape, proportion, size, packaging, use, consumption, even caloric value and many other components in play may be the same. In the case of Kinder milk slices, the symbolism of the material "milk" (baby food, white and innocent, healthy, nourishing, nutritious, good for children, etc.) is at least partly transferred to the milk slices, even though to the senses the milk filling feels very different from conventional milk.

Taste – and what it conveys

Even taste or certain types of flavor can act as a sign. Take curry, for example: by means of a very specific mixture of spices a distinctive type of taste is created which serves as a kind of trademark and gives a name to its own entire category of dishes. As with the characteristic taste of gingerbread (cinnamon, cloves, etc.), the specific taste of curry and all other foods where a special flavor (seasoning) is the key ingredient is what identifies the food itself. The taste is a signal to recognize gingerbread, curry or punch as such. What taste combinations convey, however, goes beyond simple indication. The taste of a food always acts as both a signal and as a representation (symbol). With clearly identifiable taste patterns, not only is a particular dish indicated, but also a set of associated ideas that have nothing to do with food intake per se. Associations of this kind may pertain to e.g., the recipe's country of origin, certain eating rituals or times of the day, seasons, places, situations, etc. in which eating is typical, or to subconscious, atmospheric and emotional states and contents that are difficult to put into words.

Taste combinations serve as a medium for the transmission of meaning. As long as the taste pattern itself is the carrier of meanings (that is, internalized as a symbolic form), taking the long way round via the dish is consequently no longer necessary in order for the associated ideas to be evoked. A specific taste idea – be it "curry," "gingerbread" or "punch" can be clearly identified as such and linked with its corresponding meanings, not only in connection with a specific dish but also in other spheres – in soaps, shower gels or candles, for example. It is not the dish but the taste that presents "curry" and all the ideas connected with it as an institution. A bar of soap or a candle smells of "gingerbread" and evokes an associated set of images in the brain. An ice cream tastes like "punch" and thereby evokes all its associated mental and emotional connections, although the drink itself is not in evidence.

Through taste, dishes are indicated and ideas evoked in which the two functions – signals and symbols – flow together and cannot be clearly separated. Taste combinations show that a cuisine belongs to and represents a particular group of people and their food habits. Most cuisines follow a specific formula of seasoning styles which give the dishes a distinctive combination of flavors typical of this particular cuisine, making it distinct from others.[153] Accordingly, food at its most elementary level – that of taste perception – creates identity. Taste patterns show that a dish belongs to a particular culture, and symbolize this affiliation at the same time. One example of this is chili, which is actually something we have a natural aversion to, but is nevertheless one of the most common seasonings worldwide. This penchant for chili distinguishes humans from all other omnivores, though rats can also learn to like it. The taste of chili is strictly speaking not a taste but a trigeminal irritation; i.e., liking a pain sensation is a learned response. Because it has an intense-tasting, unmistakable taste feature, it also serves to label and identify dishes belonging to a certain cuisine.[154]

If they are distinctive enough, specific taste features that are predominant in a critical number of dishes and drinks within a culture identify them as belonging to that particular culture. Once a particular taste combination or aromatic trait has been set to establish a particular context of meaning, the information can also be transferred to other (unknown) items: a dish is thus perceived to belong if it has the appropriate taste, even if it has never been eaten before. The taste therefore serves as a sign of authenticity and fulfills functions such as categorizing, orienting and differentiating. Another example is the intensely sweet tastes of North America. Many foods typical of the US such as donuts, ice cream, syrup and soft drinks primarily taste sweet; they stand out not because of any specific flavor, but because of their intense sweetness. The taste combination "extreme sweetness" thus acts as the particular feature of a certain lifestyle. Strictly speaking, it is not the material "sugar" that is an "attitude" or an "institution,"[155] but the taste of extreme sweetness.

Colors – and how they convey meaning

The colors of food serve to indicate its flavors among other things. According to its color and setting, people associate how food looks with certain tastes and effects. In an experiment, for example, test subjects associated the color green with "sour," "fresh," "healthy" and "toxic;" red with "sweet," "healthy" and "aromatic."[156] Colors are linked to certain ideas, which in turn influence the taste. For this reason, many sensory tests are performed under blue light to render the actual color of the food unrecognizable. This means that the selfsame food tastes different according to its color (as long as the food is visually perceived before eating). For instance, the impression of color has an effect on taste intensity: Cherry juice, for example, (apparently) tastes sweeter when it is colored an intense red.[157] Margarine, orange juice or raspberry jelly are perceived as being less flavor-intensive when they are colorless.[158] This effect is called "quantitative modulation"; i.e., a certain expectation intensifies or lessens a taste impression, which in this case is triggered by the color.[159]

Since color is a visual sensory stimulus that doesn't alter the chemical-physical perception of taste in the mouth and throat, the (apparent) change in taste at the cognitive level – i.e., when process-ing the sensation of taste, must therefore take place in the brain.[160] This means it is an actual change, not merely an apparent one, because taste does not in fact arise in the mouth but in the brain. The meanings and interpretations that are evoked as a consequence of the impression made by color are joined in the brain by those that are activated by the chemical-physical taste stimuli (and by those of other sensory organs) and are further processed into a coherent overall impression. In other words, how a food item tastes is not only influenced by ingredients and preparation, i.e., at the level of physics and chemistry, but also by the evocation of an idea. This could be for instance making a sugar-reduced drink not only "sweeter" by adding sweetener to it, but also by coloring it – so long as it is with the color that has the appropriate associations and the "right" symbolism. Color apparently forms an integral part of flavor in our minds. The recognition of certain flavors therefore turns out to be easier with the appropriate color (80% in a test with orange juice), while the identification of taste in colorless or color-changed drinks drops to 30%.[161] Taste, as well as the individual impressions provided by the sensory organs – be they color, smell or texture – is ultimately a sequence of ideas that are associated with a particular set of sensory stimuli and linked to symbolic forms based on experience, i.e., via processes of learning.

Color, examples: Filled baguettes and colorful salad bowls

The symbolism of color as a carrier of content is not limited to individual colors. Certain color combinations can also evoke associations. A "colorful" salad bowl, the toppings on a deep-frozen pizza or what is included in instant soups (or Ramen noodles / Pot Noodles) can be particularly appetizing if it contains red, green and yellow elements. The traffic-light combination of "green-yellow-red" is a simplification of the biological principle of eating as much variety as possible, "packaging" it into an visually recognizable feature. The message that differently colored food also contains different nutrients and thus guarantees a balanced diet is simplified and converted into the color combination "red-green-yellow." The eater is generally no longer conscious of the true context of meaning. The basic design principle of sandwiches – to choose the filling so that it boasts as many different colors as possible – is based on the same associative meaning. A monochrome roll covered with salami, red pepper and a slice of tomato looks boring and unappetizing, although it has quite a variety of tastes. On the other hand, the creative and stylistic approach of implementing a certain color code and combining the greatest possible number of elements produces the desired symbolic effect. Conversely, the actual quality of the ingredients is of secondary importance because the positive effect of color symbolism overrides the impression given by poor-quality raw materials like e.g., canned vegetables. The principle of nutrient richness is tied in with a color code, which as a visual sign is so effective that it also works with ingredients that are actually nutrient-poor – a contradiction of the basic principle.

Texture – and its symbolism

Unlike most other items, food is subject to a relatively rapid, natural process of decay. In addition to color and smell, changes in texture and consistency are other signs of this process. The tactile quality of edible items on the fingers, lips and mouth, and their chewing resistance, gives information about their freshness and edibility: a firm apple or a crunchy biscuit are fresh and fit for to be enjoyed. A soft or mushy texture is a typical sign of aging in the case of fruit or crunchy, baked goods.

In addition to its function as an indication – e.g., of being fresh or going off – texture also functions as a carrier of meaning in the symbolic sense. For Barthes, the bloody texture of the steak, and thus a quality of its consistency, forms a key factor in the myth of "steak": "Blood is visible, natural, dense, compact and at the same time cut-table." Those who eat it feel its "unmistakable pouring into the blood of the human being."[162] A bloody steak is both fluid (squishy) and firm (resistant) on the inside. Ideas associated with steak are communicated through the experience of this particular texture among others; i.e., the texture is relevant to the meaning. In the transmission of symbolic meaning, consistency also plays an important role in Beef Tartar: "The bloody mince, the gooeyness of the egg, the whole harmony of soft, living substances" form "a meaningful compendium of the images of the pre-birth."[163]

Consistency, Example: Crunchy

Textures convey meanings. "Crunchy" e.g., is a haptic state of edible items that results from baking, roasting or heating. It is associated with certain ideas independent of the other properties of the object in question. Whether we are talking about chips (crisps), waffles, cornflakes, biscuits, bread crusts, bread rolls, mixed nuts, a schnitzel, a roast chicken or a fish finger: When it cracks and crunches in the mouth, the teeth meet with a relatively strong biting resistance, and at the same time rough and hard bits slowly become soft and mushy; this process evokes certain associations. Eating crunchy food requires more physical activity than mushy food, which just needs to be swallowed. Crunchy is therefore more than an interesting texture or a tasty property – it is an expression of a process: the crushing and the active ingestion. "One can see how such a concept transcends the merely physical product; what a crunch refers to in food is an almost preternatural goodness, a certain piercing, awakening power that contrasts the soft, soothing character of sweetness."[164] The fact that hard, crunchy foods need to be processed – that is, chewed and digested – with a relatively large amount of effort by the body is reflected in the social significance of these foods. Hard and tough is therefore associated with active and masculine, crunchy with stimulating, exciting and sensual. Crunchiness is a sign of action and activity, and as a consequence is interpreted as an expression of a particular state of mind or approach to life: someone who feels tired and listless tends not to go for crunchy objects. If one is vigorous, on the other hand, one is keen to feel the anticipation before chomping into it. The physical expenditure of energy needed to digest food is related to psychic energy – inner strength – which people currently, generally speaking or as a rule, can muster in order to feed themselves. This effect is even used in psychology as a concept for distinguishing types of people ("thrill-seekers" versus people with a low sensation threshold).[165]

Consistency, Example: Creamy

In addition to "crunchy," a similar sensory sign system can also be examined around the idea of "creamy." Creaminess is a culinary ideal with the opposite effect: it means orally passive food, the consumption of which requires little effort. Creaminess is associated with feeding and caring. Soft and creamy stands for children and the sick, for filling up and indulgence.[166] A soft, mild, immediately digestible puree is the typical baby food; creamy is therefore linked to images like "mother" and "security." "Creamy" also stands for perfection: Cream represents the ideal state of a puree: it is totally uniform, with no bits or chunks. A cream is a perfect emulsion, and as such an expression of perfection and artificiality. "Creamy" is an idealized state because it demands absolute uniformity and a perfect and stable mixing ratio. Eating creamy food has such a strong, symbolic effect that it has developed into an ideal image, an end in itself, in the design of food.

A striking guiding principle in the design of food is the contrasting consistency of crunchy and creamy. It links two culinary ideals together, and through their juxtaposition also creates an interesting contrast that brings with it a many-faceted, sensory experience. Whereas poorly defined boundaries between two different textures are associated with natural decay (for example, undefined or unexpected consistencies and clear transitions between different textures cause uneasiness or disgust; e.g., when fluid collects around the edge of creamy food like puddings), distinct textures such as nuts in yogurt or fresh, crisp cornflakes in milk create excitement. The combination of crunchy and creamy is the key to the success of countless modern snacks, and rarely is a snack bar introduced these days that is without it.[167]

"Crispy" and "creamy" are culturally specific, learned culinary units and serve to express meaningful contexts that lie outside the sphere of nutrition through food. Because it is learned, the fascination for certain types of consistency can vary greatly according to culture. In Central Europe, for example, wobbly, gelatinous or slimy textures are not tactile ideals of edible objects, unlike in other parts of the world (e.g., certain parts of Asia).

Aroma

Aroma first and foremost fulfills a clear, biological function: to warn of decay. It serves to indicate what is inedible. Aroma can physically affect taste perception, since taste arises primarily through smell, but it can also do so by association; i.e., on the cognitive level. The smell of vanilla, for example, makes cream taste sweeter.[168] Objects that smell of vanilla will taste sweeter even if they actually contain no more sugar than comparable ones without vanilla's flavor.[169] This means that the smell of vanilla is associated with sweetness, probably as a result of experience. If something smells of vanilla, the brain concocts the very idea of a sweet taste, which is so clear and strong that it is enough to change the taste sensation of what has been eaten. Aromas are associated with certain learned ideas. In the case of vanilla, this means "sweetness"; i.e., vanilla symbolizes "sweetness" because vanilla does not in itself taste sweet. Even with other aromas, the idea communicated by a certain smell is enough to intensify the perception of the corresponding tastes. The smell of strawberries and oranges makes sweet dishes seem sweeter (even if they do not taste of strawberry or orange). This intensification of taste is likely to occur at the cognitive level of perception and not as a result of oral-nasal effects, since the altered perception of taste only occurs if there is a corresponding associative link between taste and smell. Since associations are primarily culturally learned, there are naturally significant differences in the taste perception of test subjects from different backgrounds.[170]

Countless further examples of how the properties of edible items communicate content could be compiled. The way in which something works or functions involves just as much symbolism as a chewing noise, which indicates for example when the food has been mashed up enough to be swallowed. How edible items are arranged on a plate – for example, whether presented in pairs as in sausages or sushi, or according to perceived value as with pieces of meat and their side dishes in the European culture – also makes a statement, such as the cutting of vegetables (e.g., carrots) into uniform cubes (frozen vegetables), into fine Julienne cuts – or if they are served whole with the green leaves intact. Further examples which could be examined in this way are e.g., the symbolism of the whole section of meat (festive roast) as opposed to one that has been chopped (minced) and reconstituted (meat loaf); or the symbolism of different processing techniques, such as spit roasting, in which the calorie-rich fat drips into the fire and burns, as opposed to the "poor man's" stews that conserve the energy value of the ingredients – and need less fuel for cooking. The portion size (such as a children's ice lolly compared to a Magnum) and the proportions (for example, the ratio of bread to topping, which, for example, in a Big Mac happens to be in favor of the topping) are also meaningful, and trigger corresponding interpretations.

Conclusion

Since the form (appearance) and thus the design, as an action that determines the form of something, cannot be separated from the object itself but defines the qualities that the senses can experience – and thus also how (or as what) something is perceived – it can be said that the form ("gestalt") determines how an object is interpreted as a sign. Because food is designed in a given way – and not another – it lays claim to a certain symbolism; i.e., it defies certain interpretations. People interact creatively with objects in two ways: firstly through interpretation – the kind of perception in which an object as such is recognized, conceptually classified, "read" and interacted with accordingly. This is how the decision of whether to eat it or not, among others, is made. And secondly – in the case of design objects, i.e. processed food – by the way it is designed. By designing things, people are constantly creating signs. The word "design" implies the activity of actually designing (the drafting process) on the one hand, and its conceptual framework (the nature of the result) – i.e., the nature of the finished product – on the other.[171] Both types of creative interaction have to do with symbolism: through the objects being read and interpreted on one hand, and through active design in the course of processing and preparation on the other. It is no accident then that the German-American designer Klaus Krippendorff, together with Reinhart Butter, coined the term "product semantics" in 1984, defining it in two ways: first as an examination of the symbolic qualities of things, and second as an active design tool.[172]

(Food) Design determines behavior

Design language is just as omnipresent in daily life as conventional language. If verbal language is the basis of communication between people, then object language is (initially) the basis of communication with the world of objects. Like spoken language, object language informs the actions and behavior of perceivers by implying or even imposing practical knowledge. Meaning is not only transmitted directly through sensory stimuli, but above all by the sorting of the same stimuli into a cultural interpretation pattern. Humans not only react to the physical properties of things – such as form, structure or function – but also to their individual and cultural meanings.[173]

Even the symbolic content that is communicated by things – that is, the higher meanings that things hold – determines behavior; i.e., is crucial for a response, not just the physical-material characteristics. In many cases, food products are – according to Eva Barlösius in any case – not evaluated as "good" or "bad" by dint of their natural (objectively measurable) properties (e.g., bitter taste, awful smell, dark, blue-black color or mushy consistency all being signs of going off), but as a result of culturally learned connotations.[174] For example, the strong "off-smell" of cheese and other fermented foods (e.g., Natto, a fermented Japanese soybean paste), the black sheen of pasta with sepia ink, the bitter taste of certain alcoholic drinks or coffee are considered tasty or enjoyable in some cultures; despite the same features acting as indicators of decay or toxicity in other contexts. Whether the pure white, sticky-soft layer of fat on meat or ham is experienced as tasty or disgusting, as pleasurable or harmful to health, is a further example of how much the interpretation and evaluation of food products depend on culturally learned associations, which are then projected onto the object's properties: If one has learned that animal fat is bad (harmful to health), the perception set by "soft, white, wobbly" is coded as "disgusting" in the context of meat.

Objects give off signals, thereby inducing certain patterns of behavior.[175] The very meaning of "edible" immediately demands specific ways of relating to the object in question. It is a clear guideline for treating the object in a particular way, i.e., unlike any "non-edible" object. The transition from passive perception to action initiated by an object is described as appropriation by German psychoanalyst Alfred Lorenzer (1922–2002), whose work was also recognized and adopted in design literature.[176] In this sense, we appropriate food twice: once as an object that gives off signs and is associated with a certain activity – for example, putting it in your mouth and biting it off – and again physically in its actual intake or ingestion. In addition to the purely physical appropriation of food, there is also an appropriation or reproduction of knowledge which is transmitted through the form during the act of eating.

Signs are learned – Eating is "educational"

Socialization through items that are directly experienced by the senses leads to an interrelation between supra-familial (for example, religious) symbolizations and the personality of the individual.[177]

155

The overwhelming share of personal knowledge (and the activities based on it) is not self-acquired experiential knowledge, but comes from others; i.e., it is socially mediated.[178] This mediation happens not only verbally but also through actions – the contact and use of objects, for instance. As a central background of experience in the daily environment, food products and how they are designed form an important part of these learning processes of socialization, contributing to the development of the individual's repertoire of knowledge and consequently to the formation of the individual personality. In the process of food design, people are automatically forced to engage with culture – i.e., the group's definitions and structures of meaning – and form an opinion accordingly. The design of food thus also works as a mediator of knowledge that "educates" the eater – directly or indirectly: Directly e.g., by showing the way in which something ought to be eaten, and indirectly by conveying the symbolic meaning of the community. If "learning processes in education are about people's interaction with cultural content and global reality as a whole,"[179] then food design forms part of such educational processes. On the one hand, this dialog actively takes place through the design of food and dishes (by introducing symbols), and on the other passively through the selection and consumption of such (by deciphering symbols), but always within the framework of the group's structures of meaning (culture). Knowledge can thereby be acquired or transmitted indirectly – through the object "food" – from others.[180] If "education" is understood to mean the "initiation of a person into his / her cultural environment"[181] as well as the reflexive processes triggered thereby, interactions with food can in any case be regarded as a (not insignificant) part of these processes.

It is people that infuse symbolism into a thing, after which it gains validity within a certain group. This group can be very small (even including only one single person, if it is for example a purely personal experience); but it can also be very large. For research into the cultural connections of food, and into its design and function as a symbol, collective signs are naturally of the greatest interest – i.e. those signs whose sphere of influence is as large as possible. The specific connections between form and content, which produce a (symbolic) sign, are socially learned. In order to correctly interpret the content and meanings of food and its forms, an appropriate prior knowledge base is necessary. In order to understand a group's symbolism, one has to know how they categorize their information into individual object characteristics. This knowledge is not only passively recalled but is also transformed and advanced with each meal. The group's members themselves produce the meaning of collectively valid signs by convention; not on the individual level but socially – i.e., from the totality of the group – and it is passed on (i.e., taught) as "culture" or "tradition" within it.

Interaction with edible items is – just as with other objects of daily use – not necessarily based in functionality, but is the result of conventions, and varies greatly from group to group. Any particular food culture is influenced by the ideology of the group and dependent on its conceptualizations, ideas and thoughts.

1 Papanek, 1984, p. 6

2 Baudy, 2008, p. 61

3 See Elschenbroich, 2010, p. 72

4 Lang, 1989, p. 7

5 See Döbler, 2000, p. 88

6 Godau, 2003, pp. 26f

7 See Schneider, 2009, pp. 11–12

8 See Barthes, 1961, p. 984

9 See. Barlösius, 1999, pp. 97–98

10 See Korsmeyer, 2002, pp. 7 and 131

11 Lorenzer, 1981, p. 18

12 Lorenzer, 1981, p. 18

13 See Korsmeyer, 2002, p. 119

14 See Knoblauch, 2005, pp. 150 and 285

15 See Vihma, 2010, p. 15

16 Vihma, 2010, pp. 13–14

17 Vihma, 2010, p. 16

18 Meier, 2001, pp. 29–30

19 See Vihma, 2010, pp. 13–14

20 See Bense, 1971, p. 22

21 Vihma, 1997, p. 35

22 Vihma, 2010, p. 15

23 See Bense, 1971, pp. 25 and 52

24 Vihma, 2010, p. 15

25 Vihma, 2010, p. 20

26 See Steffen, 2000, pp. 29 and 82

27 See Langer, 1954, pp. 23–24

28 See Langer, 1954, pp. 216–217

29 Bonsiepe, 1996, p. 233

30 See Vihma, 2007, p. 226

31 See Bürdek, 1997, pp. 6, 10, 12, and Steffen, 2000, p. 7

32 See Steffen, 2000, p. 7

33 See Krippendorff, 2006, foreword

34   Krippendorff, 2006, pp. 1–2

35   Vihma, 2007, p. 226

36   See Steffen, 2000, p. 10

37   Vihma, 1997, p. 31

38   Vihma, 1997, p. 33

39   See Vihma, 2007, p. 223

40   Vihma, 2007, p. 224

41   See Langer, 1954, pp. 78–81

42   See Langer, 1954, pp. 77–79

43   See Langer, 1954, p. 179

44   See Langer, 1954, p. 78

45   See Turner, 2012, p. 223

46   See Knoblauch, 2005, p. 148

47   See Langer, 1954, p. 58 and Spence, 2017, p. 15

48   See Collins, 2012, p. 92

49   See Langer, 1954, pp. 79–81

50   See Bense, 1971, p. 33

51   See Langer, 1954, pp. 78–80

52   Wimmer, 2005, pp. 38

53   See Langer, 1954, pp. 79–80 and Korsmeyer, 2002, p. 103

54   See Langer, 1954, p. 74

55   See Langer, 1954, p. 75

56   Knoblauch, 2005, p. 143

57   Langer, 1954, p. 80

58   See Langer, 1954, pp. 74–75

59   See Dürrschmid, 2009, p. 4

60   Barthes, 1957, Le mythe est une parole

61   See Barthes, 1957, Le mythe comme système sémiologique

62   See Knoblauch, 2005, p. 157

63   See Barthes, 1957

64   See Steffen, 2000, p. 7

65   Vihma, 2010, pp. 20, 21 and 30

66   See Steffen, 2000, p. 23

67   See Vihma, 2007, p. 224

68   See Dürrschmid, 2009, p. 4

69   See Langer, 1954, p. 212

70   See Liebau, 2008, p. 11

71   Triadic relation according to Bense, 1971, p. 22

72   See Bense, 1971, p. 36

73   See Barthes, 1957, Le bifteck et les frites

74   Blochel-Dittrich, 2009, p. 77

75   See Korsmeyer, 2002, p.139 and Blochel-Dittrich, 2009, p. 77

76   Vihma, 2007, p. 224

77   Langer, 1954, p. 63

78   Langer, 1954, p. 216

79   See Langer, 1954, p. 217

80   Barthes, 1961, p. 979

81   Barthes, 1961, p. 979

82   See Kolmer, 2008, p. 160

83   Barthes, 1961, p. 979

84   Barthes, 1961, p. 980

85   See Kogge, 2012, p. 32 and Collins, 2012, p. 93

86   See Knoblauch, 2005, p. 148

87   See Berger, Luckmann, 1989, p. 41

88   Langer, 1954, p. 72

89   See Steffen, 2000, p. 63

90   Vihma, 2010, p. 16

91   See Bense, 1971, p. 34

92   See Döbler, 2002, p. 89

93   Burgstaller, 1958, p. 166

94   See Währen, 2000, pp. 609ff

95   See Lurker, 1979, pp. 379–380

96   See Währen, 2000, p. 627

97   Sorgo, 2006, p. 263

98   See Korsmeyer, 2002, p. 129

99   See Bense, p. 36

100   Langer, 1954, p. 58

101   See Langer, 1954, pp. 72–73

102   Langer, 1954, p. 58

103   See Hirschfelder, 2001, p. 20

104   Sorgo, 2010, p. 70

105   Barlösius, 1999, p. 103

106   See Barlösius, 1999, pp. 96–97

107   Därmann, 2008, p. 20

108   Barthes, 1961, p. 977

109   Barthes, 1961, p. 977

110   See Barthes, 1961, p. 978

111   E.g., traditional sacrifice; see Mellinger, 2000, p. 76

112   See Fiddes, 1991, p. 39

113   Fiddes, 1991, p. 93

114   See Mellinger, 2000, p. 28

115   Fiddes, 1991, p. 175

116   Fiddes, 1991, p. 68

117   Fiddes, 1991, p. 66

118   See Fiddes, 1991, p. 70

119   See Mellinger, 2000, pp. 29 and 31

120   Barthes, 1957, Le bifteck et les frites

121   Fiddes, 1991, p. 65

122   See Mellinger, 2000, p. 51

123   Rigotti, 2003, p. 45

124   See Rigotti, 2003, p. 46

125   See Czerny, 2009, p. 105

126   Eder, 1988, p. 240

127   See Stummerer, Hablesreiter, 2010, p. 310

128   See Vihma, 2007, p. 224

129   See Burkard, 2011, p. 182

130   See Lorenzer, 1981, p. 20

131   See Schneider, 2009, p. 199

132   See Lorenzer, 1981, p. 20

133   See Korsmeyer, 2002, p. 125

134   See Schwendter, 1995, p. 51

135   See Enzinger, 2008, p. 36; Kolmer, 2008, pp. 115 and 117

136   See Schwendter, 1995, p. 51

137   See Schwendter, 1995, p. 51

138   Wimmer, 2005, p. 13

139   Wimmer, 2005, p. 32

140   Wimmer, 2005, p. 49

141   Barthes, 1961, p. 979

142   See Vihma, 2010, p. 20

143   See Langer, 1954, p. 79

144   See Turner, 2012, p. 228

145   Barthes, 1961, p. 981

146   See Barthes, 1961, p. 981

147   See Gniech, 2002, p. 58

148   See Dürrschmid, 2009, pp. 15–17 and Spence, 2017, p. 22

149   See Dürrschmid, 2009, p. 59

150   See Dürrschmid, 2009, p. 25

151   See Spence, 2017, p. 45

152   See Stummerer, Hablesreiter, 2010, p. 247

153   See Hahl, 2001, p. 18

154   See Hahl, 2001, p. 18

155   See Barthes, 1961, pp. 977–978

156   See Gniech, 2002, p. 59

157   see Spence, 2017, p. 41 and Gniech, 2002, p. 60

158   see Gniech, 2002, p. 61

159   see Dürrschmid, 2009, p. 19

160   see Dürrschmid, 2009, p. 20

161   see Gniech, 2002, p. 60

162   Barthes, 1957, Le bifteck et les frites

163   Barthes, 1957, Le bifteck et les frites

164   Barthes, 1961, p. 981

165   See Gniech, 2002, pp. 71–75

166   See Gniech, 2002, pp. 71–73

167   See Barthes, 1961, p. 981

168   See Dürrschmid, 2009, pp. 20–21

169   See Spence, 2017, p. 22

170   See Dürrschmid, 2009, p. 20

171   See Erlhoff, Marshall, 2008, keyword design

172   See Krippendorff, 2006, pp. 1–2

173   See Krippendorff, 2006, foreword

174   See Barlösius, 1999, p. 85 and Spence, 2017, p. 74

175   See Lorenzer, 1981, p. 158

176   See Lorenzer, 1981, p. 155 and e.g., Steffen, 2000, pp. 7 and 25ff.

177   See Lorenzer, 1981, p. 13

178   See Knoblauch, 2005, pp. 148ff

179   Wiater, 2012, p. 21

180   See Knoblauch, 2005, p. 150

181   Oelkers, 2011, p. 73

The fish finger as a case study

The premises that are placed on the design of a food product are
embedded in the socio-cultural and political arena in question. For
example, the history of how the fish finger came to be shows how
societal and political conditions influence the design of food.

A fish finger is a ca. 7.5 cm by 2.5 cm by 1.3 cm cuboid made of
deep-frozen, breaded and pre-cooked fish which is intended for consumption. Generally, the middle consists of so-called "mix blocks," i.e.,
made from fish fillet, which mostly comes from cod, hake or Alaskan
salmon, and fillet sections (V-sections), which result from boning and
are then mixed again with the original fillets.[1] The coating is made
from fried breadcrumbs, which can vary in color, thickness and granularity depending on the region. Fish fingers are exclusively produced
industrially.

Production

The fresh fish is first processed into deep-frozen blocks; the resulting
pure fish blocks are an international commodity. To get those blocks
the boned fish is usually directly separated on board the fishing vessel
into types, pressed between two plates in the so-called contact freezer
and simultaneously frozen at -30 to -40° degrees Celsius. In factories
back on land, the deep-frozen blocks are then cut with band saws
into the desired format. After that, the fingers first pass on link belts
through the wet batter, a tub filled with fluid dough, which allows
proper adhesion of the breading when passing through the breading plant. Next, the fingers are pre-cooked at about 170°C for about
20 seconds. The center of the fingers remains frozen; the breading
solidifies. The cuboids are then cooled, passed through a metal detec-
tor and packaged.[2]

How and why did this specific preparation of fish come about?

Fish fingers first appeared in the US in the 1950s. In contrast to other mass-produced foods, they did not arise as the conversion of a hand-made ("homemade") product (recipe) into mechanical manufacturing techniques – like e.g., the machine-baked roll as a mass-produced version of the hand-baked roll – but rather as a consequence of technical development and industrial food production itself. However, a recommended breakfast recipe called "Fish Fingers" – apparently with the intention of using up leftovers – actually appeared in the British magazine "The Tamworth Herald" on June 30, 1900, which reads as follows: Flake and mince any cold cooked fish very finely, and mix it with two-thirds its bulk of cold cooked rice; season to taste with pepper, salt, and minced parsley, mixing it into cakes with the white of an egg; shape these neatly, brush with beaten egg, cover with breadcrumbs, and fry in plenty of hot fat.[3] This dish was not however, to become the model for the development of today's fish fingers from breaded fish cubes.

Exactly why fish fingers are designed the way they are can be explored in two questions:

How did the design of "fish fingers" historically come about, and Why has it been maintained as a food product for several decades?

History of origin

The reason for the design of the fish finger can be explained through its historical origin. The design of fish in the form of fish fingers originated with the need for the fishing industry to sell its catch, the quotas of which had increased as a result of new technologies. Improvements in the efficiency of catching fish, thanks to larger and faster boats among other things, had enabled the fishing companies to increase their production and thus their turnover. After the Second World War, floating factories were used to process the catch directly on board. A further boost in efficiency came from the civilian use of military inventions such as the radar, which was able to locate shoals of fish in real time. Some governments, e.g., the Canadian government, subsidized these new fishing fleets in order to secure jobs in the fisheries sector.[4] In turn, the development of freezing technology had made it possible to preserve larger catches. The inventor of frozen food is American biologist Clarence Birdseye (1886–1956). Inspired by Inuit methods of freezing raw fish very quickly and at very low temperatures during a period of research in Newfoundland in the 1910s, he developed the plate freezer in the late 1920s, laying the foundations for the deep freeze industry.

The first attempts to freeze fish were unsuccessful. The fillets looked unsightly, sustained unsightly burns as a result of freezing, had a tough texture and were unpleasant-smelling. Moreover, vestiges of skin and offal often caused bacterial infections. The research undertaken in order to solve these problems showed that the speed of deep freezing has a bearing on whether the texture and other quality features of the fresh fish are preserved or not. This is because the faster the frozen food cools down in the course of deep-freezing, the smaller the ice crystals that are formed in the fish meat, allowing the cells to remain intact and the fish not to dry out. Clarence Birdseye, who had a substantial impact on the development of quick freezing, introduced frozen foods to the market from 1930 on.[5]

The fisheries industry benefited from advances in freezing technology and new fishing techniques, but found it difficult to sell ever-larger quantities of a product that was still unfamiliar to the consumer – frozen fish.[6] There are two main reasons why the fish finger was designed the way it was: a production-distribution reason and a visual-sensory one: Firstly, large-scale production of frozen fish had to solve a problem of scale: the massive, heavy blocks of fish that the catch was frozen into at sea were well-suited for industrial manipulation but not for retail sale. The attempt to separate the fish fillets that had been frozen into blocks before they were sold – fillet by fillet – failed, however: The result was tattered and unsightly units of fish that were unsuitable for sale. For the frozen fillets to be marketed, another form of portioning had to be found which divided the frozen fish into units that were small enough for further processing at home. To satisfy this requirement, the blocks were cut with band saws in the factories into geometric, but fetching and appetizing, cuboids. Although any natural clue to the raw material "fish" was lost, a novel, "clean" and pre-portioned food object was created in its place. Convenient cuboids made of frozen fish thus emerged out of a specific need for distribution and portioning.

However, because the frozen bars of fish – the so-called "fish-bricks," which were packaged in blocks similar to ice cream and intended for further processing in the kitchen – sold poorly, the sensory and functional quality of the frozen fish blocks had to be changed. The breaded and pre-cooked version of bite-sized, pre-portioned fish blocks offered several advantages: For one thing, it tasted familiar with well-known recipes such as fish and chips. Fish and Chips was created between 1840 and 1880 in Lancashire, London and Dundee and probably goes back to an even more ancient Jewish tradition of breading, frying and eating fish cold.[7] Moreover, the breaded bars proved to be an aesthetically well-received variation of frozen fish which also boasted numerous technical advantages (see below) and which no longer had to be prepared in the home kitchen – only heated.[8]

After three years of development work in Birdseye's own laboratory in Boston, the company introduced modern fish fingers (as we know them today) to the US market for the first time in October 1953. At virtually the same time, other manufacturers also entered the fish fingers market. Fish fingers became an overnight success. Within just a few months, they had reached 10% of the market share of non-canned fish products. In 1954, sales rose by a further 30%. Fish fingers also benefited from the generally rising consumption of frozen food, which had already been used in the US from the 1940s for practical reasons that in fact had to do with supply: since canned food was needed for the soldiers overseas and was therefore rationed, people switched to frozen foods.[9]

Freezing disconnected ingredients from the natural cycle of the seasons and ended eaters' seasonal dependence on their food.[10] Suddenly, fresh fish was available all year round, miles away from the coast. Fish fingers and similar products made frozen fresh fish constantly available and thus expanded the traditional food spectrum.

In addition, the consumption of fish had gained importance during the Second World War years because meat had been scarce. In the 1950s, one of the declared aims set by producers of fish was to use fish fingers in the "protein war" when meat became available again. Corresponding advertising campaigns made a big deal out of fish containing as much protein as meat but being more digestible, among other things.[11]

Technical functions

Breaded fish bars offer a series of advantages in comparison to non-breaded pieces of frozen fish, but from today's point of view it is no longer clear which of them contributed to the invention of the fish finger and which proved to be successful in the sale of the new product afterward (i.e., happened coincidentally or as a result of other criteria, without having been consciously taken into account in the design process).

These include among others:

That the breading keeps the fish in the right shape and prevents the relatively small fish pieces from crumbling while being cooked.

The breading is ideal for holding spices. In the course of industrial production, regional taste preferences (i.e., different spice mixes) can easily be catered for and adjusted despite the same production process and the same raw material (pure frozen fish blocks) being used. In addition, the need for the consumer to do the seasoning in the kitchen is eliminated. Fish fingers can therefore also be prepared by people unfamiliar with cooking.

The design of the fish fingers makes it possible to adapt to regional tastes without having to change the preparation process itself (for example, the production lines). The recipe for fish fingers, e.g., which type of fish is processed, can be varied without a great deal of technical effort. For example, there are fish fingers intended for consumption in landlocked countries where the intense aroma of marine fish is not part of the traditional range of flavors – like the more mild-tasting polar cod fillet; while in coastal regions the more intensive-tasting hake or salmon are used. Additionally, the condition of the breadcrumbs – e.g., the degree of roasting, the color shade (between yellow, orange, light and dark brown), the granularity, etc. – are easily adaptable to local culinary preferences.

The breadcrumbs prevent the individual fish fingers in the pack from freezing together, thus facilitating the pre-portioning. Fish fingers fall out of the packet one at a time and do not stick to it, unlike non-breaded frozen fish.

With pre-portioning, building block-style fish fingers can be made into any number of portions of any size (e.g., child portions, etc.). The portioning can be carried out without weighing and irrespective of package size.

Palatability: because of their pre-portioned, oblong shape, fish fingers can be easily held by hand and comfortably put in the mouth.

Fish fingers are a semi-prepared meal. The breaded fingers are relatively easy to prepare, although compared to other ready meals they need to be cooked, not just heated. However, cooking is reduced to a single process (frying or deep-frying) that needs just one pan ("heat and eat"). No further processing of the fish in the kitchen is necessary. The need to handle raw fish, which is often perceived as disgusting (keywords smell, slimy surface, fluid discharge etc.), is eliminated. The manufacturers observed that most housewives do not like handling fish and were not able to prepare it, which was considered to be the main advantage of this new fish dish.[12]

External (political) influences

The development of fish fingers in the mid-twentieth century happened due to a combination of various technological, social and political developments. Among other things, the fish finger benefited from sociological and societal changes that came about as a result of World War II. In the 1940s, ready-made products quickly gained market share as a consequence of more women entering the workforce in order to replace the men who had been conscripted as soldiers. Fish fingers were deliberately marketed at stressed and overburdened housewives among others, thereby contributing to the creation of the instant meal as a symbol of the modern lifestyle.[13]

An industrial product as symbolism

Fish fingers are a highly processed, high-tech food product. They are a product of industrial design. The generally high level of confidence in progress and technology during the space age resulted in an enthusiasm for industrial products (including edible ones) and the advantages of having ready-made meals. This fascination with progress and technology was expressed among other ways in political decisions that also benefited the fish finger. Thus, the university research necessary for perfecting freezing technology, food safety and the development of suitable frozen supermarket display cabinets was supported by the state.[14]

Politically, in the US the fish finger also consistently profited from so-called "School Lunch Programs," a state-funded, non-profit program for schoolchildren with the hidden agenda of creating an outlet for surplus agricultural produce. Since fish fingers are nutritious, considered healthy, and are also cheap to prepare with minimal effort, restaurants, hotels, caterers and schools provided a perfect market for the pre-portioned fish dish. Together with fries, they made a simple and nutritious main course. Other options for serving fish fingers were as a burger topping with tartar sauce, as a warm appetizer or with scrambled eggs as a breakfast![15]

The aesthetics of the object "fish fingers"

Fish fingers are a dish shaped by strong, aesthetic contrasts. Sensorially and symbolically, fish fingers break down into two contradictory elements: the white, soft, mild-tasting, fibrous filling that offers little biting resistance but disintegrates on the tongue, and the hard, crispy, rough, grainy, dark breadcrumbs with the intense, oily, roasted taste. In addition, the contrast between the two "soft – rough," "light – dark," "juicy – crispy," "mild – intensive," etc. is enhanced by the fact that one of the two elements completely envelops – and thus hides – the other. Only when the breadcrumbs are broken and cut (i.e., destroyed) is the second part (the fish) exposed.

Disguising the raw material

In the process of manufacturing fish fingers, the living creature "fish" is made unrecognizable. With the breadcrumbs on the one hand and the uncompromising geometric cuboid shape on the other, the base material is not visible from the outside; not even guessable. Similarly to the sausage, the high degree of processing – through filleting, boning, pressing, freezing, sawing, breading, frying etc. – leads to an aesthetic and sensory dissociation from the raw produce. The design of the fish finger is a "denial" of the raw material fish.[16]

The disassembling of food animals transforms them into "civilized," i.e., intensely man-made (art) products. Modern ready meals like fish fingers or chicken nuggets follow this principle, as do traditional, heavily processed dishes like sausages that deconstruct the meat as an ingredient into tiny parts by mincing and grinding. Generally speaking, food preparation is a form of "artificialization." Human food culture, in comparison to the animal kingdom, is automatically associated with a "denaturing" of food. Human discoveries such as fire, agriculture or sourdough alter the "natural" appearance of food.[17]

The disguising of the raw material, which automatically happens during the preparation of food and forms the basic process of any kind of cooking, also fulfills a symbolic function. Food such as fish fingers or chicken nuggets, the appearance of which does not resemble the anatomy of a chicken, are a soft, harmless and mild dish precisely because they are aesthetically disassociated from the dead animal of which they mainly comprise.

The material "fish" and its symbolism

A change in meaning occurs in the transformation from fish to fish fingers. Over the course of this process, fish fingers are aesthetically and emotionally disassociated from the creature "fish." However, this disassociation is hindered by the sensory interference factor of the aroma, which strongly smells of fish even when in the form of fish fingers. The raw substance fish is usually neither shown on the packaging nor in commercials – only the name makes any reference to the original material. Fish fingers are not disassociated from the starting material on a mental level: the term fish is kept in the name, and with it the rational intellectual meanings that fish impart (e.g., health).

Is the transfer of fish symbolism to the fish finger, which looks visually very different from a fish, allowed at all? Even if with fish fingers the raw material "fish" only reaches the table in a strongly altered state, it is still considered a fish dish. Within the framework of food, fish is the dominant ingredient in the categorization of fish fingers, as opposed to breadcrumbs which are considered more a preparation method than an ingredient. Fish fingers are perceived as a form of "fish" in spite of their dissociation from the original substance. The meanings contained within the material "fish" form part of the object fish fingers.

The fish is an ambivalent symbol. It is a strange creature, admired but also feared; peculiar and unfathomable. They are envied for their ability and freedom to move effortlessly through the three-dimensionality of water. Fish, as an important food staple in Mediterranean cultures, are a symbol of good luck similar to the pig in Central Europe; even today, both animals are used as good luck charms at New Year.[18]

On the other hand, fish are also cold, wet, slippery and silent, and live in the dark depths of the ocean. In depth psychology, they are considered to represent the precursor of human existence and are associated with the deeper levels of the psyche. There is therefore something sinister about fish. In ancient Egypt, priests and kings were forbidden from eating fish. As silent creatures that lived in the deep, they were considered eerie and associated with negative myths. On the other hand, eel, perch and other fish were revered as sacred. In Syrian rites, there were also holy fish in the cults of Artemis and Cybele, and during the great flood, fish would not have been affected by God's curse.[19]

In Christian mythology, which hails from the Mediterranean, the fish is a positive, life-affirming symbol. It stands for food. Together with bread, it is considered a symbolic representation of the divine meal and is typically the third Eucharistic dish after bread and wine in the depiction of The Last Supper.[20] It is no coincidence that fish dishes are an important part of the traditional Christmas and New Year menu.[21] In the New Testament, the symbol of the fish is representative of the miraculous feeding of the five thousand,[22] and as an allegory that Jesus used when he wanted his disciples to become "fishermen for humans."[23] The fish not only stands for food – and therefore for life – but also for Jesus Christ himself and those who follow him. It was used until the end of the 4th century as a secret mark of identification for Christians.[24]

But to what extent can the symbolism of the fish be transferred to the fish finger? The soft, white, neutral inner part of the fish finger matches the positive symbolism of the fish: free, innocent, auspicious. By removing the "dark" parts of the fish such as skin, bones, cartilage or innards, the fish loses its ambivalence. The cold, wet, slippery parts of the fish are lost. What is left is the unblemished fillet. It is 100% free of bones, uniform, perfect and entirely safe to eat. Similar to the sausage, the uniform texture assures safety from bones, cartilage or other bothersome, hard-to-digest factors. It requires no great attention or skill to eat the harmless, homogeneous, reliable and reassuring flesh. Fish fingers offer a culinary vision of an "ideal" world free of danger, and satisfy a longing for the perfect dish.

Despite the loss of its ambivalence, fish in the form of fish fingers is nevertheless still not boring. The addition of a second, artificial element averts the danger of monotony: The breadcrumbs, as a totally risk-free and harmless replacement for bone or cartilage, counteract the uniformity of the fillet. Natural animal textures such as skin, bones, etc. are removed and then added again condensed, abstracted and minimized as a "crunchy shell," so to speak. And last but not least, the breadcrumbs also carry certain symbolic meanings, like e.g., the idea of using up leftovers (bread) or the association of the golden color of breadcrumbs with the historical tradition of gilding food for representative as well as dietary purposes.[25]

The fish finger (and its specific design) is, in technological, social and political terms, an ideological representative of the industrialized system from which it emerged. On the one hand, the content communicated by the fish finger stems from its technical background, but on the other hand it is mixed in with established (already existing) symbols that can be identified in the fish finger. And finally, social, economic and political instruments, institutions and events (e.g., wars, political movements, public and scientific discourse, marketing) also have an effect on the design in that they influence the hierarchy of levels of meaning, i.e., the technical and symbolic functions and their significance.

1   See Heiss, 2004, p. 97

2   See Heiss, 2004, p. 97 and Belitz, Grosch, Schieberle, 2008, p. 651

3   See http://www.foodsofengland.co.uk/fishfingers.htm, on 4.6.2014

4   See Josephson, 2008, p. 45

5   See Josephson, 2008, pp. 44–45

6   See Josephson, 2008, pp. 41–42 and 45

7   See Davidson, 2006, p. 303 and Schwendter, 1995, p. 234

8   See Josephson, 2008, p. 45

9   See Josephson, 2008, pp. 45–53

10   See Josephson, 2008, p. 44

11   See Josephson, 2008, pp. 47–50

12   See Josephson, 2008, p. 51

13   See Josephson, 2008, pp. 47ff

14   See Josephson, 2008, pp. 42–43

15   See Josephson, 2008, pp. 51 and 57

16   See Hablesreiter, Stummerer, 2010 (2), p. 82

17   See Lemke, 2007, p. 356

18   See Biedermann, 1994

19   See Biedermann, 1994 and Thiel, 2010, p. 15

20   See Biedermann, 1994

21   See Thiel, 2010, pp. 14–15

22   Joh. 6, 1–15, Mt. 14, 16–21, Mk 6, 38–44, Lk 9, 13–17

23   Mt 4, 19, Mk 1, 17, Lk 5,10

24   See Biedermann, 1994

25   See Wagner, 1996, p. 233

Food as a means of expression and receptacle of knowledge

Eating is more than just a matter of enjoyment and taste. It is an essential feature of life itself, a bridge between life and death. If we don't eat or eat the wrong thing, we die. Food is of the highest priority in everyday life – in both a physical and metaphysical sense. The fact that food comes in so many different shapes and sizes – e.g., the variety we see in our daily bread – cannot be rationally explained. What is the point in preparing fancy dishes when a simple bowl of porridge will fill you up just as well? From a purely biological point of view, it makes no sense to go to the effort of shaping dough into a multi-looped pretzel. A pretzel feeds us no better than a loaf of plain bread. Designs that increase yield, make inedible things edible through certain preparation methods or preserve ingredients obviously improve the basic function of food. But why do people subject perfectly good raw materials to cumbersome preparation processes that serve neither their preservation nor wholesomeness, and shape them into various forms? People could feed themselves far more easily and, biologically speaking, would not live any worse if they ate only a few, very simple dishes. Why is food so varied and elaborate?

Food Design as a means of expression

Objects of all kinds and the particular way in which they are designed are a means of expressing concepts and thoughts. All humans share the drive to design (whatever); an urge that springs from the never-ending search for media through which to express ourselves. For Susanne Langer, the essence of language is generally not primarily in its function as a communication system, but as a means of formulating and expressing ideas.[1] Food, like other man-made objects, also acts as a medium of expression. Food and drinks are therefore designed the way they are also because everyday objects of all kinds – including food – offer the opportunity for such expression.

Eating culture as a form of expression

Food is – consciously or unconsciously – designed in such a way that it expresses certain concepts, meaning that it holds significance for the people concerned. For Susanne Langer, rituals – and in this sense, the design of food as the systematic implementation of an everyday basic need – are symbolically transformed experiences that cannot be expressed in any other medium than through the performative and demonstrative symbols of a ritual. According to Langer, rituals evolve among other things from the innate human need to express ideas, the urge to symbolize concepts. The design of food objects can be seen as a form of this "expressive action."[2]

If concepts and thoughts are expressed through a specific design, then the medium of expression – in this particular case food – transforms into the medium that conveys this concept. If they are personal, individual ideas, then these remain legible only to the person concerned. However, if the medium of expression "food" is used to express the combined thoughts of an entire group, e.g., if active procedures such as preparation processes and recipes are systematized and ritualized accordingly, then the relationship between certain ideas and their associated means of expression within this group is fixed (conventionalized) and the corresponding food product becomes a common carrier of meaning. The group's own eating culture then functions as a collective form of expressive action.

In addition to their traditional function (as providers of nutrition), food and drink are also a tool for expressing culture, which as a social process of negotiating meaning[3] needs to be constantly implemented in order to keep (alive) the collective fabric of meanings and thus confirm their validity. Culture specifies the common patterns, which are nevertheless reproduced in local and individual variations – though only according to the cultivated pattern – e.g., as a particular dish such as curry or bagel, in order that group-specific symbols and meanings are actually and definitively realized. Andreas Wimmer refs to such individual actions that occur within a group pattern as a "cultural compromise."[4] This performative repetition is necessary in order to store and pass on cultural knowledge; the variations in turn create space for reflection and the further evolution of the system.[5] Food design allows such expression. At the same time, the collective reproduction of the group's individual meanings through the design of food is one reason why food culture is usually considered meaningful. Ideas that are expressed collectively define community. In any case, apart from actual data content, they also convey affiliation with the respective group of people who expresses them. Food, like other community-specific systems of behavior, generates meaning because it is a collective means of expression.[6]

In addition to group affiliation, other information and all sorts of ideas can also be expressed that have little to do with nutrition, the actual purpose of food. According to Langer, magic and ritual serve to "symbolize divine presence" and formulate a religious universe.[7] Ritual foods fulfill the same purpose – in principle – as all the food objects that we are positively disposed to, that "say" something to us and thus make sense: they establish contact with our systems of meaning.

Example: Confectionery as a poem; edible verse

One example of how entire stories, situations and moods are communicated that expresses through food what makes a culture tick is the traditional Japanese tea confectionery. The shape and color of Wagashi, as they are called, either depict the beauty of nature and the particular season, correspond to a special occasion such as holidays and festivals, or reflect astronomical phenomena. Some designs also refer to poetry or traditional stories.[8] Karagoromo, for example, is a half-green, half violet-colored, round praline that refers to a poem from the Tales of Ise (a collection of 10th-century Japanese texts) set on a waterfront in early summer among the hare-eared iris blossoms. The green color of one half of the praline evokes the image of the iris leaves and the purple color of the other half symbolizes the blossoms.[9] What is fascinating about Wagashi is that a relatively simple aesthetic hint (e.g., green color) can trigger the imagination of a whole story, fairytale or myth. Wagashi are mainly made from sweetened bean curd and are traditionally eaten during the tea ceremony (Chasekigashi). Originally, the sweets also had a ritualistic character and served to ward off evil or to ask for a long, healthy life or a good harvest. Chasekigashi and Wagashi were artistically refined from the 16th century on, as the rich and varied repertoire of Wagashi in today's style gradually developed.[10] Some of today's varieties still date back to designs from this era. The elaborately designed nibbles are meant to capture the uniqueness of the moment – especially the atmosphere of the season – and thus aesthetically promote the philosophy of the tea ceremony (harmony, respect, purity and serenity).

Wakabakage, "In the shade of fresh leaves," for example, is a transparent cuboid revealing small, pale green leaves and a small goldfish on the inside. It is served in the hot and humid rainy season in June and is supposed to give the eater the refreshing sensation of cool water.[11] A similar purpose is intended with Mizu no hotori, "The Edge of the Water"; in the dumpling of green paste two marks have been pressed in the shape of expanding, circular waves. Its surface is sprinkled with dried rice cake powder. It is eaten in May at the beginning of the hot summer months and expresses the calm coolness of a shaded waterfront.[12] Saikanotsuki, "Moon over Rape Blossoms" is a yolk-yellow, round rice cracker filled with bean jam and eaten in March. It is said to represent the rising moon over a hazy, flowering rape field.[13] Iwane no tsutsuji, "Azalea at the base of a rock," consists of folded, green beans with stripes of purple bean paste in the middle symbolizing the flowering of the azalea. Azalea is viewed as a sign of late spring or early summer, and so Iwane no tstsuji is served in May.[14] Yusuzumi, "Evening Cool," is a round ball with streaks of white and pale-blue bean paste that depicts the feeling people experience outdoors on a hot August evening when the air is cooling down – to name some more examples.

Wagashi in its entirety is a culinary system the concept of which is a kind of calendar for the senses.[15] Like the sacramental wafer, the taste of Wagashi is only of secondary importance. The more than 3000 different, sometimes very elaborate designs have only a few, relatively similar tastes. The consumption of Wagashi is far more associated with spiritual rather than sensual pleasure. Eating a Wagashi is like reading a poem; it puts you in a different world for a few moments. It is the suggestions and associations evoked in the mind, rather than the sensory enjoyment of the taste, that the eater is supposed to enjoy.[16] Although Wagashi is no longer necessarily eaten as part of the tea ceremony, its design still expresses the Japanese philosophy of life.

Food Design is a means to express a philosophical-cultural attitude to life (for example, power structures and hierarchy) and to implement it on a day-to-day basis. The contents of what is expressed not only reflect the respective group's conceptual world, but also carry that group's systems of meaning (and their authentication). As a collective means of expression, the design of food contributes to the individually experienced sense of the meaning of one's own existence and the authentication of one's respective reality.[17] Design itself does not – at least on the surface – create any content, but it does act as a medium for the realization of such content, in that a particular design evokes its allocated associations and concepts. In the end, it is a question of definition whether the interlinking of content and design (appearance) to signs that are generally able to create new connections and insights is seen as generator of content, or whether the signs are merely seen as carriers of previously existing concepts and ideas. The latter assumes that the already-familiar content of an existing repertoire is evoked through a particular design. With the former, on the other hand, a novel configuration of familiar content is regarded for example as the mediation of new ideas that had not previously been in existence; that are for instance recognized and understood because of their similarity in spite of not themselves being part of the original repertoire; arising only as a result of the new association. Bense sees the introduction of a sign on the whole as a generative process ("semiosis").[18]

Food generates meaning

The design of food and drinks is not pragmatically driven as such, as the intention of design is not necessarily to make food as functional and efficient as possible, but to express ourselves and our ideas and to legitimize our own existence. As we do this, technical, economic or pragmatic efforts are made without them being justified by any (superficially) apparent reason.

Considering the work and thus the economic effort needed to form a pretzel, for example, without creating special flavors or other characteristics conducive to enjoyment leads to the notion that part of the reasoning behind the production of pretzels goes beyond nutrition, enjoyment and taste. Eating a pretzel is also mentally satisfying because it makes "sense," be it from a social, ritual, traditional, religious or other standpoint. When we satisfy our hunger, we satisfy not only a basic biological need, but also – as long as choice and availability permit – a mental one: Food that tastes good not only satisfies the stomach, but also the soul (in a symbolic, social and emotional sense).[19]

We eat first and foremost what we understand, what is in line with our ideas, what makes sense to us – not necessarily what we like. Since taste is culturally relative and people are able to acquire it, taste is neither an objective sensory impression nor an objectively describable property of an object. Instead, it – or in its negative form, disgust – functions as a mechanism for justifying patterns of behavior in order to ensure these patterns of action survive and are observed.

The selection of potential food sources, as well as the design of food products, constitute symbolic universes. Berger and Luckmann understand symbolic universes as "bodies of theoretical tradition that integrate different provinces of meaning and encompass the institutional order in a symbolic totality," wherein symbolic processes "refer to realities other than those of everyday experience." "Legitimation now takes place by means of symbolic totalities that cannot be experienced in everyday life."[20] Food products and their specific preparation or design offer people the opportunity to connect closely and daily with higher-level systems of meaning and to understand themselves as part of a larger universe, beyond their sphere of influence.[21] The function that the symbol of "food" satisfies for the individual confirms one's own symbolic universe, that which "puts everything in its right place."[22] Whenever one delves into previously unexplored experience, "the symbolic universe allows one ' to return to reality' – namely, to the reality of everyday life."[23] The symbolic universe – in this specific case the conventionalized way of designing food – gives an institutional order its ultimate legitimation.[24] The theoretical systematization of symbolic universes is what follows. The symbolic universe is thus not only legitimized, but also modified by theoretical concepts in order to resist dissidence.[25] One of these theoretical concepts is taste.

The entire nutrition system with all its sub-elements – from procurement to design (preparation) to eating rituals – forms such a symbolic universe. Within the totality of culture, the system of food and its design is actually an essential system of symbols, because every member of a group is automatically affiliated and is forced to play a part in it. One cannot escape food, and therefore the decision about which food items one incorporates into oneself and which not. The totality of all a group's eating items can be regarded as a system of meaning in whose physical creation many members participate; in whose production and evolution through the interpretive perception and daily handling however all members, with the exception of the comatose and suckling infants, participate all the time. Food is a network of meanings because we are always eating; we are interpreting edible objects.[26]

One answer to the question of why food products are designed in a specific way is that design can create a link as a medium between people and meaningful content: "Design is making sense of things."[27] Historical food offerings such as croissants or sweet breads reveal how people use design – in this case of baked goods – to evoke certain ideas and connect with a symbolic universe beyond the realities of daily life.[28]

The design of food products doesn't necessarily improve their function as providers of nutrition, but may possibly provide other functions outside the primary use value of nourishing the body. Edible objects – just like weapons, tools or items of daily use – are designed for more than their actual original purpose: "Artifacts have been embellished to make them stand out, to individualize them or to give them magical powers."[29]

One possible explanation for why some everyday objects such as certain food products are elaborately designed is so they interconnect with a common, higher-level system of thought that links groups in space and time – across a number of generations. Those (still known and practiced) examples of food design that are particularly old are of ritual origin. Certain kinds of food product - with regard to their style of design – appear to have supported certain rituals and performative practices, one of whose tasks was to create a link between different realities.[30] In order to have the desired effect, e.g., establishing contact with goddesses and gods, a certain design was apparently necessary for some food offerings – or they were meant as replicas of other offerings, i.e., substitute offerings from edible raw materials which had to have a similar form in order to be acceptable. Some examples of this are the croissant as an object for contact with moon deities; braided bread as a bakery substitute for the sacrifice of one's own hair; bread offerings in the shape of fish, which were common in ancient Egypt;[31] or the baked sacrificial lamb for Easter, in which the actual animal sacrifice was replaced by appropriately shaped loaves (or cakes).[32]

Food Design as a receptacle of knowledge

The preparation of food and drink represents knowledge that is passed on within a community from generation to generation. Dietary knowledge is probably the most ancient knowledge of all.[33] This knowledge also includes the preparation of food and other design aspects which can be preserved over generations and centuries in the form of culinary lore such as recipes, menu sequences, preparation methods or food combinations.

The collective knowledge of the ancestors, which is often encoded in culinary lore, can be passed on to the next generation through a corresponding socialization. It is applied, adapted, adjusted if necessary to changed living conditions and passed on to the next generation.[34] Each group possesses such a collective, imaginary, immaterial memory independent of the individual, capable of directing the behavior of group members and overriding biological control.[35] This extra-lingual set of rules, (tacitly) anchored in communities through social convention, forms a kind of "social" language that manifests in day-to-day modes of behavior and represents a store of "collective tacit knowledge."[36] This mass of collective, tacit knowledge, very similar in nature to language, enables symbols to be interpreted in the same way as other members of one's own community interpret them. This symbolic convention (consonance) within a particular group of people – one might also call it culture – is baffling insofar as there is something collective and implicit that is individually owned, albeit in a rudimentary form of coherence purely at the collective level and cannot be explicitly described.[37] This being the case, any research into such a store of knowledge is ultimately doomed to fail.

Culinary systems of classification

Cultural classification systems are one specific expression of this collective knowledge, which gives personal instructions for how to live and shows itself in the way we design, among other things. Culinary (and non-culinary) classification systems form a basis for how social relationships are regulated. The design classification of food is one aspect among others of how culture regulates people's lives; it determines people's relationships to each other and to nature. Rituals and belief systems, which are also enacted through food and its design, represent "the evolutionary collective consciousness of human communities."[38] These collective concepts create a sense of belonging, both temporal and spatial, and form the basis for a stable social order.[39]

One historical example of how culinary knowledge seeps into the design of food (in a certain combination of ingredients, to be specific) is the health book "Tacuinum sanitatis." The Tacuinum sanitatis dates back to the 11th century and creates a culinary classification system that continues to be of influence to this day. The book clearly shows how principles of classification can be preserved over several centuries and can influence daily life even if their underlying goals and ideals have been revised, forgotten or rendered obsolete over time; the forms that emerge from them, however, remain preserved – practically bereft of meaning. The Tacuinum sanitatis is also a tangible example of how and why specific forms of food design can come about.

Medically speaking, the Tacuinum sanitatis is based on Greek physician Hippocrates' (ca. 460 – ca. 370 B.C.) and Greco-Roman physician Galen's (129–199 A.D.) ideas about preserving health (theory of the 4 humors). The theory of the 4 humors (also known as humorism) was developed by Hippocrates around 400 B.C. as a concept of the body and disease, and is based on four humors that determine the body's state of health: yellow bile, black bile, blood and phlegm. The four humors correspond to four organs and are described with regard to temperature and humidity; they relate to the four seasons and four stages of life. The aim is to keep these four humors in a state of balance in the body. The theory was later significantly expanded upon by Galen, including four temperaments and the four elements. Historically speaking, the four-humors theory was a step forward in that it systematized the treatment of body and health and empowered individuals (or doctors) to take charge of their own state of health, so that they no longer felt at the mercy of fate and the gods. It granted people control over their own destiny. In the field of medicine, the theory of the four humors remained the definitive concept of pathology until the 19th century, albeit having been increasingly criticized in more modern times.

The ancient teachings found their way – via the detour of Arabic-scholastic health lore – into the late-medieval regimina sanitatis, a literary genre primarily concerned with healthy lifestyles, but also with healing diseases. The regimina sanitatis are based on Arabic-scholastic health lore, which in turn refers to Hippocrates and Galen. The Tacuinum sanitatis, an unusual regimen due to its tabular form and intended for practical use by laypeople, was written in Baghdad in the 11th century by a Christian doctor by the name of Ibn Butlan, who classified and translated ancient Greek texts on the topic of maintaining health.[40] In the second half of the 13th century, this tabular collection was translated into Latin. The thing that made it stand out – being written in tabular form – was a significant reason for its success and widespread circulation. By far the largest portion of the Tacuinum sanitatis deals with food and how it is consumed, how it acts and how it harms, thus forming a kind of non-binding early Codex Alimentarius since it offers advice, not legislation.[41] In terms of its content, even today's traditional Central European flavor combinations and preparation methods can be found to an extent in the Tacuinum sanitatis: for example, the principle (just a health tip, of course) of roasting (and not boiling) pork and seasoning it with mustard, a directive still observed with cold roast pork to this day. The Tacuinum sanitatis also recommends eating cream cheese with nuts, almonds or honey,[42] a combination of flavors that is appreciated with all kinds of cheeses to this day. The idea of eating whole milk with raisins can also be found today – in mushy desserts such as bread pudding or rice pudding among other things. Other combinations, on the other hand, have not survived, because for some reason they never caught on: Cucumbers with oil and honey, for example.[43]

Taste combinations and recipes as carriers of information

The Tacuinum sanitatis evaluates foods, sets out their relationship to each other and gives them a specific meaning with the intention of maintaining good health. The aim of classifying food and drink is medicinal in nature. In order for this to be optimized, a certain type of preparation, consumption and particular combinations of ingredients are recommended that subsequently shape the cultural taste. Should the original reasons for   eating cheese with honey or nuts – namely to prevent constipation – be forgotten, the combination will nevertheless survive, at least in some cases, because of tradition or convention. In such cases, however, it will simply be thought of as tasty, despite the tastiness of the combination of cheese and nuts not being rationally provable.

Taste (as a part or consequence of design) is not primarily biological, but is culturally influenced and also serves to convey information: if you eat cheese with nuts, supposedly simply because it tastes good or because you are used to doing so, you are automatically following the health regimen of the Tacuinum sanitatis without even realizing it. The knowledge of these health tips has been passed down in the form of recipes from generation to generation, but its original relationship to health has been lost. As far as the regimina are concerned, this is a positive thing: the information "eating cream cheese together with nuts or honey protects against its harmful effect (constipation)" has passed into tradition. Individuals therefore no longer need to consult the Taciunum sanitatis, but can without knowing it automatically nourish themselves properly as a result of their cultural environment. The passing on of this (originally medicinal) rule however also involves a loss of knowledge. No longer knowing that the relationship between honey and nuts is not only one of good taste but also one of maintaining good health makes it impossible for the eater to test whether their own behavior makes sense, and make amendments if necessary. Because the Taciunum sanitatis, with all its tips and rules, has at least partly been refuted or rendered obsolete by modern medical knowledge, it no longer really make any sense healthwise to continue the tradition of the recipe "cheese and nuts." Meanwhile, "cheese and nuts" has simply become just a dish that tastes (culturally) good, because this particular combination has been taught over many generations.

The way in which food is designed arises through the process of knowledge being transformed into tradition among other things. Once that knowledge has been lost, it is difficult – usually impossible – to find the original link between content and form. Systems of culinary norms, rules or codes such as recipes and cookbooks are one way of tracing back the meanings of a type of food, or the way these meanings have changed over the course of its existence. On closer inspection, the meanings often seem to make little sense, because they reflect a value system that has culturally evolved throughout history. Making sense of these "irrationalities" – the first step being the realization that these systems are not rational but cultural and traditional – can lead to new insights into the meanings behind food. The supermarket is one such example of a system of culinary codes; another is taste itself.

Food objects as repositories of knowledge

The way food products are designed can act as a store of knowledge. The accumulation of a store of knowledge which is passed on from generation to generation and is available to individuals is a selective process.[44] Behaviors, in this case styles of design, that have been tried and tested accumulate over time into cultural conventions.[45] As this process of accumulation takes place, a re-coding occurs: knowledge becomes simply rules of behavior – or design guidelines in the case of food design, e.g., cooking recipes – that have been broken down and simplified so that they are easy for each member to apply and implement in daily life. Stored knowledge is transformed into collective knowledge via a new, aesthetic level of meaning in which each member of the group participates. The content of the transmitted information doesn't necessarily have to be directly related to food, neither does it have to be dietary knowledge, but it can affect all areas of life. The advantage of design or object language over conventional language lies in the fact that knowledge that is impossible to communicate verbally can be conveyed.[46] Since most tacit knowledge does not translate into explicit knowledge and thus cannot be found in typical knowledge storage media, e.g., writing,[47] objects provide a means of communicating extra-lingual (e.g., religious or cultural) knowledge. The advantage of this kind of knowledge transfer lies in the fact that objects (as the language medium of this kind of communication) are directly experienced via the senses.[48] This is the force of aesthetic apprehension: that some truth or realization or discovery is delivered in a way that touches one intimately, that focuses and concentrates insight.[49] This means tacit knowledge can be transferred not only by persons but also by objects. The (supposed) economic disadvantage to which tacit knowledge is subject compared to explicit – namely that its mediation requires people[50] – can be toned down or balanced through the world of objects that can convey knowledge (applied by people).

Socialization through objects

This collective knowledge is transmitted through socialization, which happens not only verbally, but is also based on objects because the design and the way we use everyday things involves group knowledge and values that are learned in the process of introducing a person into the group. The socialization of individuals takes place through things; the objects contribute to participation in a group's collective memory and store of knowledge. This experience-based knowledge, which can also be stored in objects and their design, helps to realize a tried and tested way of life. Not least because of this, the objects in our environment are not only used and experienced in a practical sense, but form "the structure of our experience, the playground of a self-actualization that cannot be assessed by using the objects purely rationally or purposefully."[51]

Food Design is not only an instrument for storing a collective, partly subconscious store of knowledge over several generations, but also supports the implementation of conventionalized lifestyles, e.g., by contributing to the establishment and maintenance of contact with higher-level, immaterial value systems through the design of edible objects.

1   See Langer, 1954, p. 96

2   See Langer, 1954, pp. 39–41

3   See Wimmer, 2005, p. 13

4   See Wimmer, 2005, pp. 25ff

5   See Wimmer, 2005, p. 36

6   See Korsmeyer, 2002, pp. 8–9

7   See Langer, 1954, p.39 and Korsmeyer, 2002, p. 155

8   See Takaoka, Takahshi, Yoda, 2010, pp. 366ff

9   See Takaoka, Takahshi, Yoda, 2010, pp. 218–219

10   See Takaoka, Takahshi, Yoda, 2010, pp. 366ff

11   See Takaoka, Takahshi, Yoda, 2010, p. 228

12   See Takaoka, Takahshi, Yoda, 2010, pp. 215–217

13   See Takaoka, Takahshi, Yoda, 2010, pp. 122–124

14   See Takaoka, Takahshi, Yoda, 2010, p. 204

15   See Takaoka, Takahshi, Yoda, 2010, pp. 366ff

16   See Stummerer, Hablesreiter, 2010, pp. 289–290

17   See Lorenzer, 1981, pp. 163ff

18   See Bense, 1971, p. 36

19   See Sorgo, 2010, p. 70

20   Berger, Luckmann, 1989, p. 96

21   See Kaufmann, 2005, p. 19

22   Berger, Luckmann, 1989, p. 99

23   Berger, Luckmann, 1989, p. 99

24   See Berger, Luckmann, 1989, p. 99

25   See Berger, Luckmann, 1989, p. 107

26   See Burkard, 2011, p. 182

27   Krippendorff, 2006, foreword

28   See Sorgo, 2010, p. 70

29   Foraita, 2011, p. 51

30   See Herbig, 1988, pp. 62–63

31   See Döbler, 2000, pp. 88–89

32   See Hansen, 1968, pp. 31–33

33   See Kaufmann, 2005, p. 16

34   See Herbig, 1988, p. 71

35   See Kaufmann, 2005, p. 17

36   See Collins, 2012, pp. 105f

37   See Turner, 2012, p. 226

38   Herbig, 1988, p. 70

39   See Herbig, 1988, pp. 69–70f and 93

40   See Cogliati Arano, 1976, p. 13

41   See Cogliati Arano, 1976, pp. 32–34

42   See Cogliati Arano, 1976, pp. 104–106

43   See Cogliati Arano, 1976, p. 59

44   See Berger, Luckmann, 1989, p. 41

45   See Herbig, 1988, p. 71

46   See Schneider, 2009, p. 276

47   See Collins, 2012, p. 92

48   See Lorenzer, 1981, p. 89

49   Korsmeyer, 2002, p. 134

50   See Collins, 2012, p. 92

51   Lorenzer, 1981, p. 19

Conclusion

Whether we are talking about food or other objects, design is a medium for communicating content. Of course, the effect of food on the body is purely physical to begin with (nutritional status, health, well-being, etc.), but we are always with each meal also consuming content that connects to constellations of meaning via our cultural repertoire. Since there can be no meaningless objects, food as a thing is a means of constructing coherence and community and a means of expression. The premise on which food design is based is subject to how a given group views the world at a given place and time. Their philosophy of life is what controls the outcome of all the decisions that are made in the course of designing.

The process of design always takes place in the context of a certain state of mind and implements a certain way of life or ideology.[1] By ideology, we mean the weighing of advantages against disadvantages with regard to a specific goal. If another, more important objective appears to be a priority, certain compromises are made and undesired side effects accepted depending on one's philosophy of life, worldview etc. Even the mere evaluation of an action and its effect as an advantage or disadvantage is the result of a certain ideology – that is to say a certain attitude of mind. One example of the importance of how significant ideology (on the basis of which a certain food is created) is for assessment or classification into the current value system is seen in so-called design food: If, for example, low-fat products or fat substitutes are enhanced with carbohydrates, proteins or chemical additives,[2] this deviation from traditional production methods involving substantial technological effort is more readily accepted than if similar methods were used for economic reasons in order to produce more cheaply, using cheaper raw materials. Of course, traces of manipulation can also be detected here: different parties try to influence the perception of what is considered positive and what is not.

The objective in question

Design fulfills functions and brings certain (previously defined) goals to fruition. Which goals are pursued is a question of the ideology behind the design. The way in which we design our food not only fulfills the function of keeping the body alive, but it also implements social and cultural values into reality, because food is not only a physical but also a metaphysical building block of our very selves. On the other hand, food is also a man-made (designed) artifact and is treated as such, just like other commodities. Thus, in the western cultural sphere, the product "food" is meant to be as efficiently produced as possible, cheap, durable, hygienic, of consistent quality, etc. in order to meet the demands of modern industrial societies. The design of mass-produced food products especially has to come to terms with these two mutually contradictory value systems: Food as part of nature and its living creatures on the one hand and food as a (man-made) commodity with a certain monetary value on the other.

Studying the relationship between the design of a food product and the content it conveys reveals the motives behind its design. "By examining different reference relations, we can describe the form, recognize its qualities, and present arguments for its meaning."[3] Exploring meaning and content communicated by the way a dish or drink is designed allows taste and aesthetics to be reflected upon at a higher level. In contrast, if the design of food is merely regarded as habit or tradition, it – and the ideology communicated thereby – is accepted without reflection.

Design always takes place within a specific cultural environment. Each design works within a value system and conveys certain content that cannot correspond with the (unequivocal, absolute) truth. Design constructs reality. "Just as language creates new realities, design evokes new realities."[4] The evaluation of a design as either "good" or "bad" can only be done in relation to a particular way of thinking. Among other things, this conceptual world determines what a "function" is even considered to be, and according to which priorities they are categorized; This dependency ultimately concerns not only different ideologies but the knowledge system of an entire group, which reflects the symbolic order – or represents one of the symbolic orders – of the group in question. An important task of future food designers will be to examine, categorize and evaluate the different design functions (practical functions (technology, ergonomics, usability), aesthetic function, symbolic function, economic function, ecological function, ethical function) a food object is supposed to fulfill.

We are the outcome of our behavior. We design, produce, consume – and leave behind our waste. We follow cultural conventions – traditions, rules and laws – in all our activities. These reflect the values   of our society. Some of these cultural practices, for instance, get in the way of the idea of a sustainable[5] lifestyle and thus neglect the ecological and ethical function of design: For example, the notion that a meal which uses as many dishes as possible is particularly elegant and classy; or the belief that it is rude to serve leftovers, embarrassing to share portions, and pack or give away scraps; or that a steak tastes better and is healthier than a stew made of offal, and that meat is more valuable than vegetables in any case.

In the course of designing our food, we also decide which "materials" to use and which values we prioritize with regard to the quality and production conditions of these raw materials, i.e., ingredients.[6] We have a particular responsibility here as designers, because we stand at the interface between production and consumption: The materials that are used, and how and where they are prepared, is part of the design process. For our planet and its inhabitants (i.e., we ourselves), it matters whether designers decide on production methods that are monocultural, centralized, industrialized; or ones that are for the common good, that are democratic and sustainable. The production of food consumes a tremendous share of natural resources. Agriculture itself consumes about 70% of the world's fresh water supply and accounts for around 30% of total CO$_2$ emissions.[7] In addition, around 53% of the land area of the earth which is not covered by ice is used for agricultural purposes, making it the "agricultural footprint" of humans on the earth. Lastly, up to 40% of food is thrown away in Europe.

How a society handles "its" objects is a political question. Every product is the sum of the raw materials used in its production, the effort invested in its manufacture and all subsequent effects from production to disposal. What design can offer the world of food is an introspection (and adaptation) of the aims of the design as well as a trade-off and decision about how to prioritize interests, motivations and goals. The requirement for design to actually be able to fulfill these tasks is to have certain expectations of the design itself, as well as the possibility of allowing any reflections in terms of objectives and implementing them if necessary – in other words, a political claim to the design on the one hand and to the group in which it operates on the other. Design – including Food Design – is political because it intervenes in the world. This requires the designer to have a political attitude.[8] (Food) Design is always linked to the existing physical and metaphysical order and therefore – consciously or unconsciously – always acts in socio-political terms: Although design is not usually associated with politics and it is, in fact, profoundly political. And design gives material form and directionality to the ideological embodiment of a particular politics.[9]

Analyzing the parameters, objectives, and ideologies underlying Food Design is what generates the knowledge and scope to alter them. This knowledge contributes to the enrichment of society and to the empowerment of those who eat in terms of their food. Addressing the question of why food is designed in a particular way and not in another is helpful in examining, and if necessary adapting, design premises (e.g., functions that an object should fulfill) and their importance. A reflective, objective discourse on the design of food can help to advance knowledge of the goals of Food Design and to empower a more qualified assessment of food.

Knowledge alone is not enough to bring about action, however, because people predominantly act emotionally, socially and culturally, not rationally.[10] In the vast majority of actions and objects, the implicit, i.e., subconscious content far outweighs the explicit, pronounced content. For example, we all know that too much meat is unhealthy, bad for the climate and for ecological preservation, that it causes animal and social suffering, and yet many of us find it difficult to do without. This is not because we need it physically, but because our eating culture affords meat a very high priority. Design has the creative power to shift values   and meanings through the medium of aesthetics, however. I'm not suggesting that this is easy – but it is possible. For example, Modernism succeeded in liberating itself from the aesthetic – and thus also from the political norms – of historicism by developing a completely new aesthetic. At that time, this new aesthetic went beyond what had previously been conceivable, and thus also established an entirely new (political) claim to design and to the object itself. The shifting of meanings through creative application is the very essence of design.

Design is the content AND the medium

As (food) designers, it is our duty to examine goals and values behind the design of food and to keep on exploring the limits of our food culture. Plucking the strings of meanings and conventions also means doing away with some common types of behavior and creating opportunities for new things. In particular, food is often only perceived from one perspective; more as "nature" and less as designable . To understand that the world is malleable and to constantly strive for what is right (that which makes sense to us) – and to resist being passive against what is considered a given, or what is fated (immutable), but also convention if it has become obsolete – is a fundamental characteristic of life itself. To see the world as something that can be designed gives everyone more leeway by not adopting the status quo or the arguments and decisions of others without challenge.

The notion that food and food culture is designable is an empowering one. To understand food as designable empowers us to design it according to our goals. In this context, power can be seen as a collective form of action or as an organized plurality of action. The shapes of food such as e.g., bagels or pretzels have over time become established within a certain group, and are not only an expression of a cultural tradition, but also of a collective action that exerts power over the individual since they cannot be influenced or changed individually; only collectively. The design of food often concerns collective forms of design. Seen in this way, design can be viewed as a network of relationships between active people, manifesting itself in material objects – food. This is the pivotal point for designers: because they have the power to intercede in this network of relationships, to change and shape it, not just intellectually but sensorially, aesthetically and emotionally: Design infuses the world with meaning.[11]

Ultimately, it is about the further development of culture and the establishment of new, up to date goals. With regard to food, these goals include for example those of conserving resources, conserving land, water and climate, and respecting human rights.

One "new" design ambition could be to question the goals of progress and reject the idea of progress as an end in itself, for instance. Through design, a new understanding of progress could be formulated; not the kind of progress that is beholden to economic growth or technological innovation and considers it a sign of progress to be able to buy grapes in the supermarket in spring; rather a societal progress that is measured by its social and cultural development. In fact, it seems we have somehow lost sight of our priorities with regard to progress. Devising goals for a new kind of progress that will improve the lives of as many people as possible is, in our view, currently one of the most pressing political challenges that design has any kind of stake in. It involves thinking beyond what is currently conceivable, devising (designing) the future, conceiving and developing scenarios that manage day-to-day matters in a different way, and creatively manifesting the outcome. The German social psychologist Harald Welzer correctly thinks that the environmental movement has not been able to develop its own aesthetics up to this point:[12] "Until today, opposing the aesthetic of consumption with another, more attractive one has not been successfully achieved. For example, an aesthetic of informal common […]."[13] Every aesthetic communicates content. If goals are to be envisioned and new values   established, this new "narrative" will need its own form of aesthetics in order for it to become emotionally and culturally anchored. Design can cast meaning and content into an aesthetic so that this narrative (value system, state of mind) becomes directly tangible, comprehensible and legible in sensory and emotional terms. Knowledge alone does not lead to appropriate action – this requires a corresponding culture, the development of which is a key task of design. Conceiving of an aesthetic that narrates and "embodies" a believable and positive worldview as a universal social goal that replaces progress as a universal corporate goal is one of the most prevalent and urgent design tasks of our time. Freedom in the future cannot exist without Sustainment being made sovereign and this imposition has to be by design.[14]

"Culture is the center stage on which we negotiate our society today. Culture is the space in which different concepts of what culture is meet or collide with each other."[15] With this passage, the Austrian philosopher Isolde Charim summarizes one of the central tasks of design today. Eating is a deeply political act. With every bite we change the world: ecologically, economically and socially. The task of design in relation to food is to reflect on and adapt or redefine the ideologies underlying the design and production of food from within a larger (social, ecological, etc.) context. The demand on "good" design is at least in the equal fulfillment of economic, social and environmental needs. As designers, we can stick to conventional values – or create new ones. With these values we as a culture/society – define our relationship to nature, to our fellow human beings and to our future as human beings.

1   See Fry, 2011, p. 6

2   See Gniech, 2002, p. 127

3   Vihma, 1997, p. 35

4   Bonsiepe, 1996, p. 233

5   The term "sustainability" comes from the German "Nachhaltigkeit" which related to farmers stocking up for the winter. It was first mentioned in writing in 1713 by Hans Carl von Carlowitz in connection with the consumption of firewood for silver mining: Carlowitz used "Nachhaltigkeit" ("sustainability" in German) to describe the principle according to which only as much wood should be felled as reforestation is able to replenish it. The aim was to sustain the long-term profitability of silver mining. Today's definitions of the term essentially refer to the definition of "Sustainable Development" from the United Nations' 1987 Brundtland Report. According to this report, sustainability is based on a balanced interaction of ecological, economic and social considerations.

6   See Fry, 2011, p. 235

7   See Borries, 2016, p. 30

9   Fry, 2011, p. 6

10   See Welzer, 2019, p. 63

11   See Fry, 2011, pp. 6 and 239

12   See Welzer, 2019, p. 58

13   Welzer, 2019, p. 96

14   Fry, 2011, p. 186

15   See Charim, 2018, p. 95

Bibliography

Abel, Günter, Zeichen- und Interpretationsphilosophie der Bilder, in Bredekamp, Horst, Werner, Gabriele, Bildwelten des Wissens, Kunsthistorisches Jahrbuch für Bildkritik, Vol. 1.1, Akademie Verlag, 2003, pp. 89–102

Aicher, Ottl, Zeichensysteme der visuellen Kommunikation, Alexander Koch, 1977

Ainsworth, Mark, Fish and Seafood, Identification, Fabrication, Utilization, Delmar, Cengage, Learning, NY, 2009

Antonelli, Paola, Design bites, in Catterall, Claire (ed.), Food, Design & Culture, Laurence King, London, 1999, pp. 54–63

Barilla, Guido, Pasta, History, Technologies and Secrets of Italian Tradition, Barilla Alimentare, Parma, 2001

Barlösius, Eva, Soziologie des Essens, Eine sozial- und kulturwissenschaftliche Einführung in die Ernährungsforschung, Juventa Verlag, Weinheim und München, 1999

Barthes, Roland, Mythologies, Editions du Seuil, Paris, 1957 (Mythologies, Paladin, London, 1972)

Barthes, Roland, Pour une psycho-sociologie de l'alimentation contemporaine, Annales. Histoire, Sciences Sociales, 10/1961, Vol.16(5), pp. 977–986 (Toward a Psychosociology of Contemporary Food Consumption, in Counihan, Carole, Van Esterik, Penny, Food and Culture, Routledge, New York, 2013, pp. 23–30)

Barthes, Roland, Writing Degree Zero & Elements of Semiology, Jonathan Cape, London, 1967

Barthes, Roland, L´empire des signes, Skira, Geneva, 1970

Baudrillard, Jean, Le système des objets, Gallimard, Paris, 1968 (The System of Objects, Verso, 2006)

Baudy, Gerhard, Heiliges Fleisch und sozialer Leib, Ritualfiktion in antiker Opferpraxis und christlicher Eucharistie in Gottwald, Franz-Theo, Kolmer, Lothar (ed.), Speiserituale, Essen, Trinken, Sakralität, S. Hirzel Verlag, Stuttgart, 2005

Baudy, Gerhard, Zum Brotessen verdammt – durch Brot erlöst, in Därmann Iris, Lemke, Harald (ed.), Die Tischgesellschaft, Philosophische und kulturwissenschaftliche Annäherungen, Transcript Verlag, Bielefeld, 2008, pp. 61–86

Bauer-Wabnegg, Walter, Kleine Welten, Design muss auch in Zukunft Geschichten erzählen können, in formdiskurs, Journal of Design and Design Theory, 3, II, 1997

Beaumont, Thierry de, Culinary Design's free eaters, in Design Culinaire, le manifeste, Ecole Supérieure d'Art et de Design, Reims, 2004

Belitz, Hans-Dieter, Grosch, Werner, Schieberle, Peter, Lehrbuch der Lebensmittelchemie, Springer-Verlag, Berlin Heidelberg, 2008

Ben-Yossef, No'am (Hsg.), Bread, Daily and Divine, Catalogue No. 523, The Israel Museum, Jerusalem, 2006

Bense, Max, Zeichen und Design, Semiotische Ästhetik, Agis, Baden-Baden, 1971

Berger, Peter L., Luckmann, Thomas, The Social Construction of Reality, Anchor Books, New York, 1989

Biedermann, Hans, Knaurs Lexikon der Symbole, Droemer Knaur, Munich, 1994

Birus, Thomas, Landwirtschaft und Ernährung, in Brockhaus Mensch, Natur, Technik, Band: Mensch, Maschinen, Mechanismen, Leipzig, Mannheim, 2000

Biswas, Ramesh K., Mattl, Siegfried, Davis-Sulikowski, Ulrike, Götterspeisen, Springer, Wien, 1997

Blochel-Dittrich, Iris, Die Hostie, in Friedlander, Michal, Kugelmann, Cilly (ed.), Koscher & Co., Über Essen und Religion, Jüdisches Museum Berlin, Nicolai, Berlin, 2009, pp. 74–77

Bonsiepe, Gui, Interface. Design neu begreifen, Bollmann, Mannheim, 1996 (Interface – An Approach to Design, Jan Van Eyck Akademie, Maastricht, 1998)

Borries, Friedrich von, Weltentwerfen, Eine politische Designtheorie, edition suhrkamp, Suhrkamp, Berlin, 2016

Boudan, Christian, Géopolitique du gout, La guerre culinaire, Presses Universitaires de France – PUF, Paris, 2004

Bourdieu, Pierre, La Distinction, Critique sociale du jugement, edition de minuit, Paris, 1979 (Distinction, A Social Critique of the Judgement of Taste, Routledge, London 2015)

Brandes, Uta, Design ist keine Kunst, Kulturelle und technologische Implikationen der Formgebung, Lindinger und Schmid, Regensburg, 1997

Brandes, Uta, Stich, Sonja, Wender, Miriam, Design durch Gebrauch, Birkhäuser, Basel, 2009

Braudel, Fernand, Civilization and Capitalism, 15th–18th Century, Harper and Row, New York, 1981–84

Bretillot, Marc, Design Culinaire, l'Atelier, Ecole Supérieur d'Art et de Design, Reims, 2006

Bretillot, Marc, Culinaire design, mode d'emploi, in Design Culinaire, le manifeste, Ecole Supérieure d'Art et de Design, Reims, 2004

Brillat-Savarin, Jean Anthèlme, La Physiologie du goût, Primento Digital Publishing, Cork, 2015 (The Physiology of Taste, Penguin Books, London, 1970)

Böhme, Hartmut, Einführung in die Ästhetik, Paragrana 4 (1995) I, Akademie Verlag, 1995, pp. 240–254

Bompas, Sam, Parr, Harry, Jelly with Bompas & Parr, Pavilion Books, London, 2010

Borka, Max, Form will follow Foquismo, in MAP Mapping The Design World, Liege, 2012

Brugger, Ingried, Eipeldauer, Heike, Augenschmaus, vom Essen im Stillleben, Prestel, München, 2010

Bürdek, Bernhard E., Design. Geschichte, Theorie und Praxis der Produktgestaltung, Birkhäuser, Köln, 1991

Bürdek, Bernhard E., Über Sprache, Gegenstände und Design, in formdiskurs, Journal of Design and Design Theory, 3, II, 1997

Bureaux, Stephane, Tool's Food, 2007

Burgstaller, Ernst, Österreichisches Festtagsgebäck, Eigenverlag der Bundesinnung der Bäcker, Wien, 1958

Burkard, Franz-Peter, Anthropologie der Religionen, J.H. Röll, Dettelbach, 2011

Burkert, Walter, Wilder Ursprung, Opferritual und Mythos bei den Griechen, Wagenbach, Berlin, 1990

Camporesi, Piero, Odori e sapori, introduction to Corbin, Alain, Storia sociale degli odori. XVIII e XIX secolo, Mondadori, Milano, 2005

Carter, David E., Branding, Hearst Books, New York, 1999

Catterall, Claire (ed.), Food, Design & Culture, Laurence King, London, 1999

Charim, Isolde, Ich und die Anderen, Wie die neue Pluralisierung uns alle verändert, Paul Zsolnay Verlag, Wien, 2018

Chevalier, Jean, Dictionnaire des symbols, mythes, rêves, coutumes, gestes, formes, figures, couleurs, nombres, Laffont, Paris, 1993

Chow, Rosan, What Should be Done with the Different Versions of Research-Through-Design, Transcript Verlag, 2010

Christopher, Alexander, Notes on the Synthesis of Form, Harvard University Press, Cambridge MA and London, 1964, edition 1971

Classen, Constanze, Howes, David, Synnot, Anthony, Aroma, The cultural history of smell, Routldege, London, 1994

Cogliati Arano, Luisa, Tacuinum Sanitatis, Electa, Milano, 1973

Collins, Harry M., Tacit and Explicit Knowledge, University of Chicago Press, Chicago 2010

Collins, Harry, Drei Arten impliziten Wissens, in Loenhoff, Jens (ed.), Implizites Wissen, Epistemologische und handlungstheoretische Perspektiven, Velbrück Wissenschaft, Weilerswist, 2012, pp. 91–107

Cooper, Robert G., Winning at New Products, Accelerating the Process from Idea to Launch, Perseus Publishing, Cambridge, Massachusetts, 2001

Csikszentmihalyi, Mihaly, Rochberg-Halton, Eugene, The meaning of things, domestic symbols and the self, Cambridge University Press, Cambridge, 2002

Czerny, Ilonka, Fleisches-Lust – Lust auf Fleisch, in Journal Culinaire, Nr.09, 2009, Edition Wurzer & Vilgis, 2009, pp. 105–111

Därmann, Iris, Lemke, Harald (ed.), Die Tischgesellschaft, Philosophische und kulturwissenschaftliche Annäherungen, Transcript Verlag, Bielefeld, 2008

Därmann, Iris, Die Tischgesellschaft. Zur Einführung, in Därmann, Iris, Lemke, Harald (ed.), Die Tischgesellschaft, Philosophische und kulturwissenschaftliche Annäherungen, Transcript Verlag, Bielefeld, 2008, pp. 15–42

Davidson, Alan, The Oxford Companion to FOOD, Second edition, Oxford University Press Inc., New York, 2006

DGS, Deutsche Gesellschaft für Semiotik, Repräsentation - Virtualität – Praxis, 13. Internationaler Semiotik-Kongress 2011 in Potsdam, Universität Potsdam, Potsdam 2011

Diaconu, Madalina, Tasten, Riechen, Schmecken, Eine Ästhetik der anästhesierten Sinne, Königshausen und Neumann, Würzburg, 2005

Döbler, Hannsferdinand, Kochkünste und Tafelfreuden, Orbis, München, 2002

Dörpinghaus, Andreas, Bildung, in Horn Klaus-Peter, Kemnitz, Heidemarie, Marotzki, Winfried, Sandfuchs, Uwe (ed.), Lexikon Erziehungswissenschaft, KLE Band 1, Verlag Julius Klinkhardt, Bad Heilbrunn, 2012, pp. 154–156

Dong, Andy, The Language of Design, Theory and Computation, Springer, Wien New York, 2009

Douglas, Mary, Natural Symbols, Explorations in Cosmology, Barrie & Jenkins, London, 1973

Dürrschmid, Klaus, Gustatorische Wahrnehmungen gezielt abwandeln, Behr's Verlag, Hamburg, 2009

Drobnick, Jim, Smell Culture, Berg Publisher, Oxford, 2006

Duden, Band 7, Etymologie, Herkunftswörterbuch der deutschen Sprache, Dudenverlag, Mannheim, 1989

Eco, Umberto, La struttura assente, Bompiani, Milano, 1968 (The Absent Structure)

Eder, Klaus, Die Vergesellschaftung der Natur, Suhrkamp Verlag, Frankfurt am Main, 1988

Eisele, Petra, Bürdek, Bernhard E. (ed.), Design, Anfang des 21. Jh., Avedition, Ludwigsburg, 2011

Elias, Norbert, The civilizing process : the development of manners, changes in the code of conduct and feeling in early modern times, Urizen Books, New York, 1978

Elias, Norbert, The symbol theory, Sage Publ., London, 1995

Elschenbroich, Donata, Die Dinge, Expeditionen zu den Gegenständen des täglichen Lebens, Verlag Antje Kunstmann, München, 2010

Engelhardt Dietrich von, Wild, Rainer (ed.), Geschmackskulturen, Vom Dialog der Sinne beim Essen und Trinken, Campus, Frankfurt am Main, 2005

Enzinger, Katharina, Die Bestimmung der Serviette ist die, nicht geschont zu werden!, in Kolmer, Lothar (ed.), Finger fertig, Eine Kulturgeschichte der Serviette, LIT Verlag, Wien 2008, pp. 15–48

Erlhoff, Michael, Marshall, Tim (ed.), Design Dictionary, Perspectives on Design Terminology, Board of international Research in Design (BIRD), Birkhäuser, Basel, 2008

Escoffier, Auguste, A Guide to Modern Cookery, Heinemann, London, 1974

Feuerbach, Ludwig, Über Spiritualismus und Materialismus, besonders in Beziehung auf die Willensfreiheit, in Feuerbach, Ludwig, Gesammelte Werke, Bd. IV, Berlin, 1982

Feuerbach, Ludwig, Das Geheimnis des Opfers oder Der Mensch ist, was er isst, in Feuerbach, Ludwig, Gesammelte Werke, Bd. XII, Berlin 1982

Fiddes, Nick, Meat, a natural symbol, Routledge, London, New York, 1991

Findeli, Alain, Searching for Design Research Questions: Some Conceptual Clarifications, in Chow, Rosan, Jonas, Wolfgang, Joost, Gesche (ed.), Questions, Hypotheses & Conjectures. Discussions on Projects by Early Stage and Senior Design Researchers, iUniverse, New York, 2010, pp. 286–303

Foerster, Heinz von, Understanding understanding : essays on cybernetics and cognition, Springer, New York, 2003

Foraita, Sabine, Grenzgänge. Über das Verhältnis von Kunst und Design, in Eisele, Petra, Bürdek, Bernhard E. (ed.), Design, Anfang des 21. Jh., Avedition, Ludwigsburg, 2011, pp. 44–55

Foulcault, Michel, Les mots et les choses. Une archéologie des sciences humaines, Éditions Gallimard, Paris, 1966

Friedlander, Michal, Kugelmann, Cilly (ed.), Koscher & Co., Über Essen und Religion, Jüdisches Museum Berlin, Nicolai, Berlin, 2009

Fry, Tony, Design as Politics, Berg, Oxford, New York, 2011

Fry, Tony, Design Futuring, Sustainability, Ethics and New Practice, Bloomsbury Academic, London, 2016

Furthmayr-Schuh, Annelies, Postmoderne Ernährung, Food- Design statt Eßkultur TRIAS Thieme Hippokrates Enke, Stuttgart, 1993

Glasersfeld, Ernst von, Radical constructivism: a way of knowing and learning, Falmer, London, 1995

Glasersfeld, Ernst von, Konstruktion der Wirklichkeit und des Begriffs der Objektivität, in Gumin, Heinz, Meier, Heinrich (ed.), Einführung in den Konstruktivismus, Piper, München, 2009, pp. 9–40

Gloy, Karen, Lippe, Rudolf zur (ed.), Weisheit – Wissen – Information, V&R unipress, Göttingen, 2005

Gniech, Gisla, Essen und Psyche Über Hunger und Sattheit, Genuss und Kultur, Springer, Berlin, 2002

Godau, Marion, Produktdesign, Eine Einführung mit Beispielen aus der Praxis, Edition form, Birkhäuser, Basel, 2003

Gosling, Sam, snoop, What your stuff says about you, profile books ltd, surrey, 2008

Gottwald, Franz-Theo, Kolmer, Lothar (ed.), Speiserituale, Essen, Trinken, Sakralität, S. Hirzel Verlag, Stuttgart, 2005

Grigorieva, Alexandra, Sugar Cubes, in Goldstein, Darra (ed.), The Oxford Companion to Sugar and Sweets, Oxford University Press, New York, 2015, pp. 678–680

Grimm, Jacob und Wilhelm, Deutsches Wörterbuch, Hirzel, Leipzig 1897, Nachdruck Deutscher Taschenbuch Verlag, München, 1984

Gros, Jochen, Design im Vorzeichen der Digitale, Hochschule für Gestaltung Offenbach, Offenbach am Main, 1990

Guixé, Martí, 1:1, 010 Publishers, Rotterdam, 2002

Guixé, Martí, Food Designing, Corraini Edizioni, Mantova, 2010

Hablesreiter, Martin, Die Welt mit dem Mund erkunden, erschienen am 23./24.10.2010 in der Wiener Zeitung, Beilage Extra pp. 1–2

Hablesreiter, Martin, Stummerer, Sonja, Food Design, Über Formgebung und Gestaltung von Esswaren, in Heistinger, Andrea, Ingruber, Daniela (ed.), Esskulturen, Gutes Essen in Zeiten mobiler Zutaten, Mandelbaum Verlag, Wien, 2010 (2), pp. 66–89

Hahl, Angelika, Nahrungsmittelpräferenzen nach Paul Rozin, Grin, München, 2001

Hansen, Hans Jürgen, Kunstgeschichte des Backwerks, Gerhard Stalling Verlag, Hamburg, 1968

Harrison, Robert, The Dominion of the Dead, The University of Chicago Press, Chicago and London, 2003

Heeschen, Volker, Semiotische Aspekte der Ethnologie: Ethnosemiotik, in Semiotics, Posner, Roland, Robering, Klaus, Sebeok, Thomas A., Berlin, New York ,Walter de Gruyter, 2003 , p. 3278; chapter 156

Heiduck, Karin, Über den Geschmack – physiologisch und ästhetisch, Grin Verlag, München, 2008

Heistinger, Andrea, Ingruber, Daniela (ed.), Esskulturen, Gutes Essen in Zeiten mobiler Zutaten, Mandelbaum Verlag, Wien, 2010

Heiss, Rudolf (ed.), Lebensmitteltechnologie, Biotechnologische, chemische, mechanische und thermische Verfahren der Lebensmittelverarbeitung, Springer Verlag, Berlin, Heidelberg, New York, 2004

Herbig, Jost, Nahrung für die Götter, Die kulturelle Neuerschaffung der Welt durch den Menschen, Hanser Verlag, München Wien, 1988

Hirschfelder, Gunther, Europäische Esskultur Geschichte der Ernährung von der Steinzeit bis heute, Campus, Frankfurt am Main 2001

Hollein, Hans, Design, MAN transFORMS, Konzepte einer Ausstellung, Löcker Verlag, Wien 1989

Hörz, Herbert, Liebscher, Heinz, Löther, Rolf, Wollgast, Siegfried (ed.), Philosophie und Naturwissenschaften, Wörterbuch zu den philosophischen Fragen der Naturwissenschaften, Dietz Verlag, Berlin, 1983

Hürlimann, Annemarie, Reininghaus, Alexandra, Mäßig und Gefräßig, MAK-Österreichisches Museum für angewandte Kunst, Wien, 1996

Jacob, Heinrich Eduard, Sechstausend Jahre Brot, Rowohlt, Hamburg, 1954

Davidson, Alan, Jaine, Tom (ed.), The Oxford Companion to Food, Oxford University Press, Oxford, 2006

Jonas, Wolfgang, Research through Design through research, A cybernetic model of designing design foundations, Emerald, Kybernetes Vol. 36, No. 9/10, 2007, pp. 1362–1380

Joost, Gesche, Design als Rhetorik, Semiotik im Design, Birkhäuser, Basel, 2008

Josephson, Paul, The Ocean's Hot Dog, in Technology and Culture, Volume 49, Number 1, January 2008, The Johns Hopkins University Press, 2008, pp. 41–61

Jung, Carl Gustav, Franz, Marie-Louise von, Freeman, John (ed.), Man and his symbols, aldus Books, London, 1964

Jung, Carl Gustav, Archetypen, Deutscher Taschenbuch Verlag, München, 2001

Jütte, Robert, Vom Notwendigkeitsgeschmack zum Einheitsaroma. Prolegomena zu einer Sinnesgeschichte im 20. Jahrhundert, in Engelhardt Dietrich von, Wild, Rainer (ed.), Geschmackskulturen, Vom Dialog der Sinne beim Essen und Trinken, Campus, New York, Frankfurt am Main, 2005, pp. 47–58

Karmasin, Helene, Die geheime Botschaft unserer Speisen, Kunstmann, München, 2000

Kaufmann, Jean-Claude, Casseroles, amour et crises. Ce que cuisiner veut dire, Armand Collin, Paris, 2005 (The Meaning of Cooking, Polity Press, Cambridge, 2010)

Klanten, Robert, Ehmann, Sven, Moreno, Shonquis, Schulze, Floyd, Wagner, Ole, Raymond, Martin, Sanderson, Chris (ed.), Create, eating design and future food, Gestalten, Berlin, 2008

Knoblauch, Hubert, Wissenssoziologie, UVK Verlagsgesellschaft, Konstanz, 2005

Kogge, Werner, Empeiría, in Loenhoff, Jens (ed.), Implizites Wissen, Epistemologische und handlungstheoretische Perspektiven, Velbrück Wissenschaft, Weilerswist, 2012, pp. 31–48

Kolmer, Lothar (ed.), Finger fertig, Eine Kulturgeschichte der Serviette, LIT Verlag, Wien, 2008

Kolmer, Lothar, Tranchieren, Servieren – Studieren!, in Kolmer, Lothar (ed.), Finger fertig, Eine Kulturgeschichte der Serviette, LIT Verlag, Wien, 2008, pp. 105–132

Kolmer, Lothar, "a+2b": Der Aufbau des Mahles, heute und früher, in Kolmer, Lothar (ed.), Finger fertig, Eine Kulturgeschichte der Serviette, LIT Verlag, Wien, 2008, pp. 145–164

Korsmeyer, Carolyn, Making sense of taste, Food and Philosophy, Cornell University Press, Ithaca, 2002

Korsmeyer, Carolyn, The Taste Culture Reader, Experiencing Food and Drink, Berg Publisher, Oxford, 2005

Krippendorff, Klaus, The semantic turn, a new foundation for design, Taylor & Francis Boca Raton, London, New York, 2006

Krippendorff, Klaus, Design Research, an Oxymorgon? in Michel, Ralf (ed.), Design research now, Birkhäuser, Basel, 2007, pp. 67–80

Kubelka, Peter, Architektur und Speisenbau, in Der Architekt, der Koch und der gute Geschmack, Herausgegeben für die Akademie der Architekten- und Stadtplanerkammer Hessen, Birkhäuser, Basel, 2007 pp. 14–21

Kwiatkowski, Gerhard (Redaktionsleitung), Redaktion für Philosophie des Bibliographischen Instituts Mannheims (ed.), Meyers kleines Lexikon Philosophie, Verlag Bibliographisches Institut, Mannheim, 1987

Lang, Alfred, Vorwort zu Csikszentmihalyi, Mihaly, Rochberg-Halton, Der Sinn der Dinge, Das Selbst und die Symbole des Wohnbereichs, Psychologie Verlags Union, München-Weinheim, 1989

Langer, Susanne K., Philosophy in a New Key, A Study in the Symbolism of Reason, Rite and Art, Mentor Book, New American Library, New York, 1954

Lemke, Harald, Ethik des Essens, Eine Einführung in die Gastrosophie, Akademie Verlag, Berlin, 2007

Lemke, Harald, Die Kunst des Essens, Eine Ästhetik des kulinarischen Geschmacks, Transcript, Bielefeld, 2007

Lemke, Harald, Welt-Essen und Globale Tischgesellschaft. Rezepte für eine gastrosophische Ethik und Politik, in Därmann Iris, Lemke, Harald (ed.), Die Tischgesellschaft, Philosophische und kulturwissenschaftliche Annäherungen, Transcript Verlag, Bielefeld, 2008, pp. 213–230

Lemke, Harald, Zur Metaphysik des einverleibten Anderen, in Kimmich, Dorothee, Schahadat, Schamma (ed.), Essen, Zeitschrift für Kulturwissenschaften 1/2012, Transcript, Bielefeld, 2012

Lentz, Carola, The Porrigde debate, Grain, Nutrition and forgotten Food Preparation Techniques, in Changing Food Habits, Harwood Academic Publishers, Australia, 1999

Levine, Ed, War das Leben besser, als Bagels kleiner waren? In Friedlander, Michal, Kugelmann, Cilly (ed.), Koscher & Co., Über Essen und Religion, Jüdisches Museum Berlin, Nicolai, Berlin, 2009, pp. 66–67

Lévi-Strauss, Claude, Mythologica 1, Le cru et le cuit, Plon, Paris, 1964

Lévi-Strauss, Claude, Mythologica 3, L' origine des manières de table, Plon, Paris, 1968

Liebau, Eckart, Zirfas, Jörg (ed.), Die Sinne und die Künste, Perspektiven ästhetischer Bildung, transcript, 2008

Löbach, Bernd, Kritische Designtheorie, Aufsätze und Vorträge 1972-2000, Designbuch Verlag, Cremlingen 2001

Loenhoff, Jens (ed.), Implizites Wissen, Epistemologische und handlungstheoretische Perspektiven, Velbrück Wissenschaft, Weilerswist, 2012

Lorenzer, Alfred, Das Konzil der Buchhalter, Die Zerstörung der Sinnlichkeit, eine Religionskritik, Europäische Verlagsanstalt, Frankfurt am Main, 1981

Lurker, Manfred (ed.), Wörterbuch der Symbolik, Alfred Körner Verlag, Stuttgart, 1979

Meier, Cordula (ed.), Design Theorie, Beiträge zu einer Disziplin, Anabas, Frankfurt am Main, 2001

Meier, Cordula, Plüm, Kerstin, Die Theorie und Praxis der Dekonstruktion, in Denken nach Derrida, Beiträge zu einem Kulturphänomen, I.K.U.D. Zeitschrift für Kunst und Designwissenschaft, Band 1, Köln, 2005

Mellinger, Nan, Fleisch, Ursprung und Wandel einer Lust, Campus, Frankfurt am Main, 2000

Mennell, Stephen, All Manners of Food. Eating and Taste in England and France from the Middle Ages to the Present, Basil Blackwell, Oxford, New York, 1985

Michel, Ralf (ed.), Design research now, Birkhäuser, Basel, 2007

Miller, Jeff, Deutsch, Jonathan, Food Studies, An Introduction to Research Methods, Berg-Publisher, 2009

Montanari, Massimo, La fame e l'abbondanza, Laterza, Rom, 1993

Morel, Andreas, Der gedeckte Tisch, Zur Geschichte der Tafelkultur, Punktum, Zürich, 2001

Moulin, Leo, Le Liturgies de la Table, Mercatorfonds, Antwerpen, 1988

Müller, Klaus E., Nektar und Ambrosia, C.H. Beck, München, 2003

Mutterthaler, Roswitha, Limbeck-Lilienau, Elisabeth und Zuna-Kratky, Gabriele, Geschmacksache, Was Essen zum Genuss macht, Technischen Museums Wien, Wien, 2008

Neumann, Gerhard, Wierlacher, Alois, Teuteberg, Hans Jürgen (ed.), Kulturthema Essen, Ansichten und Problemfelder, Akademie Verlag, Berlin, 1993

Neumann, Gerhard, Jede Nahrung ist ein Symbol, Umrisse einer Kulturwissenschaft des Essens, in Neumann, Gerhard, Wierlacher, Alois, Teuteberg, Hans Jürgen (ed.), Kulturthema Essen, Ansichten und Problemfelder, Akademie Verlag, Berlin, 1993

Oelkers, Jürgen, Bildung, in Reinalter, Helmut, Brenner, Peter J. (ed.), Lexikon der Geisteswissenschaften, Böhlau Verlag, Wien, Köln, Weimar, 2011, pp. 72–79

Paczensky, Gert von, Dünnebier, Anna, Kulturgeschichte des Essens und Trinkens, Orbis Verlag, München, 1999

Papanek, Victor, Design for the real world, Thames and Hudson, London, 1984

Parasecoli, Fabio, Scholliers, Peter, Cultural History of Food, Berg, Oxford, 2012

Plattig, Karl-Heinz, Spürnasen und Feinschmecker, Die chemischen Sinne des Menschen, Springer Verlag, Berlin Heidelberg, 1995

Pollio, Marcus Vitruvius De architectura, On architecture, Ten Books on Architecture, 30–15 BC, see Rowland, Ingrid D., Howe, Thomas Noble (ed.), Vitruvius, Ten Books on Architecture, Cambridge University Press, Cambridge 1999

Prahl, Hans-Werner, Setzwein, Monika, Soziologie der Ernährung, Leske und Budrich Verlag, Opladen, 1999

Ptach, Cornelia, Köstlicher Geschmack, Umami in aller Munde, in Journal Culinaire, Edition Wurzer & Vilgis, Nr. 7, 2008, pp. 36–41

Pudel, Volker, Sicherheit und Lebensqualität durch sensorische Lust, in Engelhardt Dietrich von, Wild, Rainer (ed.), Geschmackskulturen, Vom Dialog der Sinne beim Essen und Trinken, Campus, New York, Frankfurt am Main, 2005, pp. 59–72

Rigotti, Francesca, La filosofia in cucina. Piccola critica della ragion culinaria, Il Mulino, Bologna, 1999

Röttgers, Kurt, Kritik der kulinarischen Vernunft, Ein Menü der Sinne nach Kant, transcript Verlag, Bielefeld, 2009

Schilling, Barbara, Tischkultur in der bürgerlichen Gesellschaft des 19. Jahrhunderts, Grin Verlag, München, 2007

Schneider, Beat, Design eine Einführung, Birkhäuser, Basel, 2009

Schwendter, Rolf, Arme essen, Reiche speisen, Neuere Sozialgeschichte der zentraleuropäischen Gastronomie, Promedia, Wien, 1995

Selle, Gert, Design-Geschichte in Deutschland, Produktkultur als Entwurf und Erfahrung, DuMont, Köln, 1990

Serres, Michel, Les cinq sens, Philosophie des corps mêlés, Éditions Grasset, 1985

Simon, Herbert, The Sciences of the Artificial, The MIT Press, Cambridge (MA), 1969

Skone, James, Vortrag "Social Design – Empowering the Users" held on 16.03.2010 in Vienna, Forum, Umweltbildung

Soentgen, Jens, Die Faszination der Materialien, Was Stoffe vermitteln, in formdiskurs, Journal of Design and Design Theory, 3, II, 1997

Sorgo, Gabriele, Abendmahl in Teufels Küche, Über die Mysterien der Warenwelt, Styria, Wien, 2006

Sorgo, Gabriele, Die Einverleibung der Welt, in Brugger, Ingried, Eipeldauer, Heike, Augenschmaus, vom Essen im Stillleben, Prestel, München, 2010, pp. 68–79

Sorgo, Gabriele, Konsum – die große Mutter, in Heistinger, Andrea, Ingruber, Daniela (ed.), Esskulturen, Gutes Essen in Zeiten mobiler Zutaten, Mandelbaum Verlag, Wien, 2010 (2), pp. 46–65

Spelsberg, Gerd, Essen aus dem Genlabor, Über die Zukunft unserer Ernährung, Verlag die Werkstatt, Göttingen, 1993

Spence, Charles, Gastrophysics, The New Science of Eating, Viking, Penguin Random House UK, London, 2017

Stano, Simona, Eating the Other, Translations of the Culinary Code, Cambrige Scholars Publishing, Newcastle upon Tyne, 2015

Steffen, Dagmar (ed.), Welche Dinge braucht der Mensch, Anabas Verlag, Gießen, 1995

Steffen, Dagmar, Zur Theorie der Produktsprache, in formdiskurs, Journal of Design and Design Theory, 3, II, 1997

Steffen, Dagmar, Design als Produktsprache, Der "Offenbacher Ansatz" in Theorie und Praxis, Verlag form theorie, Frankfurt am Main, 2000

Stummerer, Sonja, Hablesreiter, Martin, Food Design, Von der Funktion zum Genuss, Springer, Wien, New York, 2005

Stummerer, Sonja, Hablesreiter, Martin, Food Design XL, Springer, Wien, New York, 2010

Stummerer, Sonja, Hablesreiter, Martin, Mehr Genuss durch Food Design?, in Dr. Rainer Wild-Stiftung (ed.), Käsebrot mit Marmelade – Geschmack ist mehr als schmecken, Dr. Rainer Wild- Stiftung, Heidelberg, 2013, pp. 161–170

Sudjic, Deyan, Foreword, in Catterall, Claire (ed.), Food, Design & Culture, Laurence King, London, 1999, p. 6

Takaoka, Kazuya, Takahshi, Mutsuo, Yoda, Hiroshi, Wagashi, The graphics of Japanese Confection, Pie Books, Tokyo, 2010

Tenorth, Heinz-Elmar, Bildung, in Tenorth, Heinz-Elmar, Tippelt, Rudolf (ed.), Lexikon Pädagogik, Beltz Verlag, Weinheim und Basel, 2012, pp. 92–95

Teuteberg, Hans Jürgen, Wiegelmann, Günter, Unsere tägliche Kost, Geschichte und regionale Prägung, Studien zur Geschichte des Alltags, Band 6, F. Coppenrath Münster, 1986

Teuteberg, Hans Jürgen (ed.), Essen und kulturelle Identität, Akademie Verlag, Berlin, 1997

Thallemer, Axel, Natur und Technik. Eine neue Einheit! in Eisele, Petra, Bürdek, Bernhard E. (ed.), Design, Anfang des 21. Jh., Avedition, Ludwigsburg, 2011, pp. 212–223

Thiel, Roger, Ichthys, Annäherung an den Fisch zwischen Speise und Symbol, Journal Culinaire, Nr.11, 2010, Edition Wurzer & Vilgis, 2010, pp. 10–15

Thimm, Utz, Wellmann Karl-Heinz (ed.), Essen ist menschlich, Zur Nahrungskultur der Gegenwart, Suhrkamp, Frankfurt am Main, 2003

Turner, Stephen, The social theory of practices: tradition, tacit knowledge and presuppositions, Polity Press, Cambridge, 1994

Turner, Stephen, Implizites Wissen und das System der Spiegelneuronen, in Loenhoff, Jens (ed.), Implizites Wissen, Epistemologische und handlungstheoretische Perspektiven, Velbrück Wissenschaft, Weilerswist, 2012, pp. 215–243

Van den Boom, Holger, Betrifft: Design. Unterwegs zur Designwissenschaft in fünf Gedankengängen, Braunschweig, 1994

Vihma, Susann, Products as Representations, University of Art and Design Helsinki, 1st edition, Helsinki, 1995

Vihma, Susann, Semantic qualities in design, in formdiskurs, Journal of Design and Design Theory, 3, II, 1997, pp. 28–41

Vihma, Susann, Ways of Interpreting Design, in Strandman, Pia (ed.), No Guru, No Method?, Discussion on Art and Design Research, Aalto University School of Art and Design, Helsinki, 1998, pp. 7–13

Vihma, Susann, Design Semiotics – Institutional Experiences and an Initiative for a Semiotic Theory of Form, in Michel, Ralf (ed.), Design research now, Birkhäuser, Basel, 2007, pp. 219–232

Vihma, Susann, On Design Semiotics in Vihma Susann (ed.), Design Semiotics in Use, Aalto University School of Art and Design, Publication Series A 100, Helsinki, 2010, pp. 10–22

Vilgis, Thomas, Geschmackswahrnehmung, in Journal Culinaire, Edition Wurzer & Vilgis, Nr. 7, 2008, pp. 20–28

Vogelzang, Marije, Schouwenberg, Louise, EAT LOVE, BIS Publisher B.V., Amsterdam, 2011

Wagner, Christoph, Prato, Die gute alte Küche, Pichler Verlag, Wien, 2006

Wagner, Christoph, Das Lexikon der Wiener Küche, Deuticke, Wien, 1996

Währen, Max, Gesammelte Aufsätze und Studien zur Brot- und Gebäckkunde und -geschichte 1940–1999, edited by Hermann Eiselen, Deutsches Brotmuseum Ulm, 2000

Walker, John A., Design history and the history of design, Pluto Press, London, 1989

Watzlawick, Paul, Wirklichkeitsanpassung oder angepasste "Wirklichkeit"? Konstruktivismus und Psychotherapie, in Gumin, Heinz, Meier, Heinrich (ed.), Einführung in den Konstruktivismus, Piper, München, 2009, pp. 89–108

Wehr, Christian, Lexikon des Aberglaubens, Wilhelm Heyne, München, 1991

Weingart, Peter, Carrier, Martin, Krohn, Wolfgang, Nachrichten aus der Wissensgesellschaft, Analysen zur Veränderung der Wissenschaft, Velbrück Wissenschaft, Weilerswist, 2007

Welzer, Harald, Alles könnte anders sein, Eine Gesellschaftsutopie für freie Menschen, S.Fischer Verlag GmbH, Frankfurt am Main, 2019

Wiater, Werner, Grundbegriffe Bildung und Erziehung, in Sandfuchs, Uwe, Melzer, Wolfgang, Dühlmeier, Bernd, Rausch, Adly (ed.), Handbuch Erziehung, Verlag Julius Klinkhardt, Bad Heilbrunn, 2012, pp. 18–21

Wimmer, Andreas, Kultur als Prozess, Zur Dynamik des Aushandelns von Bedeutungen, VS Verlag der Sozialwissenschaften, Wiesbaden, 2005

Wrangham, Richard, Catching Fire, How Cooking Made Us Human, Basic Books, New York, 2009

Abbreviations

b.   born
e.g.,   for example
etc.   and so on
f.   and the following page
ff.   and the following pages
i.e.,   that is
p.   page

Square brackets within a quote indicate a note from the author/s. German quotations have been translated by Alun Brown.

Photographs

cover photography: Ulrike Köb
p. 6, 17, 22, 56, 94, 164, 177, 178, 196, 205: Ulrike Köb
p. 18, 221: honey & bunny, "food RULES tomorrow", video installation, Victoria & Albert Museum, London 2019, photograph: Sebastian Arlamovsky
p. 30: Ludwig Löckinger
p. 56: honey & bunny, "digestion design", for Vienna Design Week 2018, in cooperation with Zuckerlwerkstatt Wien, photo: Ulrike Köb
p. 157 and inside cover: Daisuke Akita

Authors

Sonja Stummerer studied architecture at the University of Applied
Arts in Vienna, the Elisava Design School in Barcelona and the
Architectural Association in London. In 2016 she gained her PhD in
interdisciplinary studies (title "food design"). Martin Hablesreiter
studied architecture at the University of Applied Arts in Vienna
and the Bartlett School of Architecture in London. After graduation
Stummerer and Hablesreiter both worked at Arata Isozaki Associates
in Tokyo, before founding the transdisciplinary studio honey & bunny
in Vienna in 2003.

They have participated as designers, performers and eat art
artists in numerous international events and exhibitions: among
others at the Victoria & Albert Museum in London, the Museo
Leonardo Da Vinci in Milan, the Museum of Applied Arts in Vienna,
the Museum of the Image in Breda (Netherlands), the Museum for
Contemporary Art and design in Trapholt (Denmark), the Designhuis
in Eindhoven (Netherlands), the August Kestner Museum in Hannover
(Germany), the Museum Bärengasse in Zurich, the Art Biennale in
Gwangju (Korea), the What Design can do Conference in Amsterdam,
the Design Indaba Conference in Capetown (South Africa), and the
Paris, Zagreb and Vienna Design Weeks. They directed the documen-
tary film "food design" for the Franco-German television network
ARTE, and curated the exhibition "food design" at the Designforum in
the MuseumsQuartier, Vienna.

Stummerer and Hablesreiter have given many international
talks, were visiting professors in Bucharest (Romania), Istanbul
(Turkey), and Chennai (India), were heads of the unit for sustainable
food design at the New Design University St. Pölten (Austria) and
currently teach at the Johannes Kepler University in Linz (Austria),
the University of Salzburg (Austria) and the Master in Food Design
program at Estoril Higher Institute in Lisbon (Portugal).

Publications (selection)

"Food Design XL," Springer Vienna/New York, 2010

"Eat Design," Metro Verlag Vienna, 2013

"Play with your Food" in Catherine Flood and May Rosenthal Sloan (ed.), Food: Bigger than the Plate, Victoria & Albert Museum, V&A Publishing, London, 2019, pp. 138–145

"Food Design: Symbols of our daily nutrition" in Simona Stano (ed.), Semiotica, Semiotics of Food, 2016 issue 211, DeGruyter, Berlin/Boston, 2016, pp. 355–369

"On designing and consuming values" in Claudia Banz and Sabine Schulze (ed.), Food Revolution 5.0: Design for Tomorrow's Society, Museum für Kunst und Gewerbe, Hamburg, Kettler, Dortmund, 2017, pp. 130–136

honey & bunny

honey & bunny is a transdisciplinary studio collective. Founded in 2003 by the architects Sonja Stummerer and Martin Hablesreiter, honey & bunny's work is situated at the intersection of research and design. Science and art are united by a thirst for knowledge and the urge to make a change. They aim to identify problems, to single them out and to address them. They have realized projects in many formats, such as performatively, publicly, digitally, while always remaining as political as possible.

honey & bunny is concerned with subjects connected to everyday life. They understand everyday actions and objects as the cradle of our existence. Culture, politics, society and the pressing issues of the present are reflected in seemingly banal objects and commonplace routines. In their eyes the exploration and the artistic handling of everyday objects such as food, cleaning agents or household tools is an essential means of provoking dialogue and interaction. If society demands a serious approach to social and environmental sustainability, it first requires cultural access to everyday life.

Sometimes honey & bunny clean houses, randomly moving from one to the next. Sometimes they use a supermarket or a coffee house when it is busiest, or they work together in a garden center with scientists and performers. They have transformed the Raphael Gallery in London's Victoria & Albert Museum into an interactive living and dining room, acted as exhibits themselves or had their work eaten by visitors of the Vienna Museum of Applied Arts. With their projects they want to touch people on an emotional level and provoke reactions. Research and performance are central to their processes of both understanding and acting. honey & bunny work at the interface between theory, science, various art forms and public participation.

food design XL

Springer-Verlag, Vienna, 2010
ISBN 978-3-99043-314-0

Why are pizzas round and fish sticks square?
"food design XL" analyzes how the design of foods is influenced by form, color, smell, consistency, chewing sounds, production technique, history and stories. More than a thousand times a year – before each meal – we cut, cook, stir or combine, that is to say deliberately change the edible gifts of nature. Our will to design food is what distinguishes us from all other living beings. Food design is thus nothing new but something the human race has been practicing for millennia.
This book traces the parameters constituting food design. Consumers expect food to be simple to produce and easy to transport, to fulfill various functions and to look good as well. "food design XL" makes the case for a discipline of design that has not received the attention it deserves to date.

eat design

Metro Verlag, Vienna, 2013
ISBN 978-3-99300-152-0

Why do we spoon our soup when we could drink it straight from the bowl? Why do we eat sitting on chairs and not on the floor? And why do we wear tight, uncomfortable clothing instead of aprons or bathrobes?
How we eat is not biologically predetermined but culturally managed. Using examples such as the spoon, the saucer, or the clinical atmosphere of fast-food restaurants, "Eat Design" documents why in the context of food intake certain things and concepts have survived over time – and others haven't.
From table tools to eating utensils to interior decoration and dress codes, "Eat Design" explores the dining act in all its design facets and shows how the objects in our eating environment control our behavior.